Cassandra 3.x High Availability

Second Edition

Achieve scalability and high availability without compromising on performance

Robbie Strickland

[PACKT] PUBLISHING

BIRMINGHAM - MUMBAI

Cassandra 3.x High Availability

Second Edition

First published: December 2014

Second edition: August 2016

Production reference: 1250816

Published by Packt Publishing Ltd.
Livery Place
35 Livery Street
Birmingham
B3 2PB, UK.
ISBN 978-1-78646-210-7

www.packtpub.com

Credits

Author

Robbie Strickland

Reviewer

Jimmy Mårdell

Commissioning Editor

Veena Pagare

Acquisition Editor

Divya Poojari

Content Development Editor

Mayur Pawanikar

Technical Editor

Suwarna Patil

Copy Editor

Safis Editing

Vikrant Phadke

Project Coordinator

Nidhi Joshi

Proofreader

Safis Editing

Indexer

Aishwarya Gangawane

Graphics

Disha Haria

Production Coordinator

Arvindkumar Gupta

About the Author

Robbie Strickland has been involved in the Apache Cassandra project since 2010, and he initially went to production with the 0.5 release. He has made numerous contributions over the years, including work on drivers for C# and Scala and multiple contributions to the core Cassandra codebase. In 2013 he became the very first certified Cassandra developer, and in 2014 DataStax selected him as an Apache Cassandra MVP.

Robbie has been an active speaker and writer in the Cassandra community and is the founder of the Atlanta Cassandra Users Group. Other examples of his writing can be found on the DataStax blog, and he has presented numerous webinars and conference talks over the years.

About the Reviewer

Jimmy Mårdell is a senior software engineer and Cassandra contributor who has worked with Cassandra for more than 5 years. He has been leading the database infrastructure team at Spotify, focusing on improving the Cassandra ecosystem at Spotify and empowering other teams to operate large-scale Cassandra clusters. He has been a speaker at many Cassandra events and in 2015 he was elected by DataStax as an Apache Cassandra MVP. Besides Cassandra, Jimmy likes algorithms and competitive programming and won the programming competition Google Code Jam in 2003.

www.PacktPub.com

eBooks, discount offers, and more

Did you know that Packt offers eBook versions of every book published, with PDF and ePub files available? You can upgrade to the eBook version at www.PacktPub.com and as a print book customer, you are entitled to a discount on the eBook copy. Get in touch with us at customercare@packtpub.com for more details.

At www.PacktPub.com, you can also read a collection of free technical articles, sign up for a range of free newsletters and receive exclusive discounts and offers on Packt books and eBooks.

https://www2.packtpub.com/books/subscription/packtlib

Do you need instant solutions to your IT questions? PacktLib is Packt's online digital book library. Here, you can search, access, and read Packt's entire library of books.

Why subscribe?

- Fully searchable across every book published by Packt
- Copy and paste, print, and bookmark content
- On demand and accessible via a web browser

Table of Contents

Preface

Cassandra is a fantastic data store and certainly well suited as the foundation of a highly available system. In fact, it was built just for such a purpose: to handle Facebook's messaging service. But it hasn't always been so easy to use, with its early Thrift interface and unfamiliar data model causing many potential users to pause—and in many cases for a good reason.

Fortunately, Cassandra has matured substantially over the last few years. I used to advise people only to use Cassandra if nothing else would do the job because the learning curve was quite steep. Version 3.x continues this trend, with the introduction of features such as materialized views and SASI indexes. These additions reduce developer workload and significantly increase the overall utility of the system.

The flip side is that each new feature further obscures the underlying data structure, making complex operations seem straightforward. The familiarity of a SQL-like interface can lure an unsuspecting new user into dangerous traps. The moral of this story is that it's still not a relational database, and you still need to know what it's doing under the hood.

And imparting that knowledge is the core objective of this book. Each chapter attempts to demystify the inner workings of Cassandra so that you're no longer working blindly against a black box data store. You will learn to configure, design, and build your system based on a fundamentally solid foundation.

The good news is that Cassandra makes the task of building massively scalable and incredibly reliable systems relatively straightforward, presuming you understand how to partner with it to achieve these goals.

Since you are reading this book, I presume you are either already using Cassandra or planning to do so, and that you're interested in building a highly available system on top of it. If so, I am confident that you will meet with success if you follow the principles and guidelines offered in the chapters that follow.

What this book covers

Chapter 1, *Cassandra's Approach to High Availability*, is an introduction to concepts related to system availability and the problems that have been encountered historically when trying to make data stores highly available. The chapter outlines Cassandra's solutions to these problems.

Chapter 2, *Data Distribution*, outlines the core mechanisms that underlie Cassandra's distributed hash table model, including consistent hashing and partitioner implementations.

Chapter 3, *Replication*, offers an in-depth look at the data replication architecture used in Cassandra, with a focus on the relationship between consistency levels and replication factor.

Chapter 4, *Data Centers*, provides you with a thorough understanding of Cassandra's robust data center replication capabilities, including deployment on EC2 and building separate clusters for analysis using Hadoop or Spark.

Chapter 5, *Scaling Out*, is a discussion of the tools, processes, and general guidance needed to properly increase the size of your cluster.

Chapter 6, *High Availability Features in the Native Java Client*, covers the new native Java driver and its availability-related features. We'll discuss node discovery, cluster-aware load balancing, automatic failover, and other important concepts.

Chapter 7, *Modeling for Availability*, discusses the important concepts readers need to understand when modeling highly available data in Cassandra. CQL, keys, wide rows, and denormalization are among the topics that will be covered.

Chapter 8, *Anti-Patterns*, complements the data modeling chapter by presenting a set of common anti-patterns that proliferate among inexperienced Cassandra developers. Some patterns include queues, joins, high delete volumes, and high-cardinality secondary indexes, among others.

Chapter 9, *Failing Gracefully*, helps you understand how to deal with the various failure cases, as failure in a large distributed system is inevitable. We'll examine a number of possible failure scenarios, how to detect them, and how to resolve them.

What you need for this book

This book assumes you have access to a running Cassandra installation that is at least as new as release 3.0. Some features discussed will apply only to 3.8 or newer, and we will point these out when that applies. Users of versions older than 3.0 can still gain a lot from the content, but there will be some portions that do not directly translate to those versions.

For Chapter 6, *High Availability Features in the Native Java Client* coverage of the Java driver, you will need the Java Development Kit 1.8 and a suitable text editor to write Java code. All command line examples assume a Linux environment, through translation to a Windows environment should be straightforward for those users.

Who this book is for

This book is for developers and system administrators who are interested in building an advanced understanding of Cassandra's internals for the purpose of deploying high-availability services, using it as a backing data store. This is not an introduction to Cassandra, so those who are completely new would be well served to find a suitable tutorial before diving into this book.

Conventions

In this book, you will find a number of text styles that distinguish between different kinds of information. Here are some examples of these styles and an explanation of their meaning.

Code words in text, database table names, folder names, filenames, file extensions, pathnames, dummy URLs, user input, and Twitter handles are shown as follows: "We can include other contexts through the use of the `include` directive."

A block of code is set as follows:

```
CREATE KEYSPACE AddressBook
  WITH REPLICATION = {
    'class' : 'SimpleStrategy',
    'replication_factor' : 3
  };
```

Any command-line input or output is written as follows:

```
# nodetool status
```

New terms and important words are shown in bold. Words that you see on the screen, for example, in menus or dialog boxes, appear in the text like this: "click on the **Connect** button."

Warnings or important notes appear in a box like this.

Tips and tricks appear like this.

Reader feedback

Feedback from our readers is always welcome. Let us know what you think about this book-what you liked or disliked. Reader feedback is important for us as it helps us develop titles that you will really get the most out of. To send us general feedback, simply e-mail feedback@packtpub.com, and mention the book's title in the subject of your message. If there is a topic that you have expertise in and you are interested in either writing or contributing to a book, see our author guide at www.packtpub.com/authors.

Customer support

Now that you are the proud owner of a Packt book, we have a number of things to help you to get the most from your purchase.

Downloading the example code

You can download the example code files for this book from your account at http://www.packtpub.com. If you purchased this book elsewhere, you can visit http://www.packtpub.com/support and register to have the files e-mailed directly to you.

You can download the code files by following these steps:

1. Log in or register to our website using your e-mail address and password.
2. Hover the mouse pointer on the **SUPPORT** tab at the top.
3. Click on **Code Downloads & Errata**.
4. Enter the name of the book in the **Search** box.
5. Select the book for which you're looking to download the code files.
6. Choose from the drop-down menu where you purchased this book from.
7. Click on **Code Download**.

Once the file is downloaded, please make sure that you unzip or extract the folder using the latest version of:

- WinRAR / 7-Zip for Windows
- Zipeg / iZip / UnRarX for Mac
- 7-Zip / PeaZip for Linux

The code bundle for the book is also hosted on GitHub at `https://github.com/PacktPubl ishing/Cassandra-3x-High-Availability-Second-Edition`. We also have other code bundles from our rich catalog of books and videos available at `https://github.com/Packt Publishing/`. Check them out!

Errata

Although we have taken every care to ensure the accuracy of our content, mistakes do happen. If you find a mistake in one of our books-maybe a mistake in the text or the code-we would be grateful if you could report this to us. By doing so, you can save other readers from frustration and help us improve subsequent versions of this book. If you find any errata, please report them by visiting `http://www.packtpub.com/submit-errata`, selecting your book, clicking on the **Errata Submission Form** link, and entering the details of your errata. Once your errata are verified, your submission will be accepted and the errata will be uploaded to our website or added to any list of existing errata under the Errata section of that title.

To view the previously submitted errata, go to `https://www.packtpub.com/books/conten t/support` and enter the name of the book in the search field. The required information will appear under the **Errata** section.

Piracy

Piracy of copyrighted material on the Internet is an ongoing problem across all media. At Packt, we take the protection of our copyright and licenses very seriously. If you come across any illegal copies of our works in any form on the Internet, please provide us with the location address or website name immediately so that we can pursue a remedy.

Please contact us at `copyright@packtpub.com` with a link to the suspected pirated material.

We appreciate your help in protecting our authors and our ability to bring you valuable content.

Questions

If you have a problem with any aspect of this book, you can contact us at `questions@packtpub.com`, and we will do our best to address the problem.

1

Cassandra's Approach to High Availability

What does it mean for a data store to be highly available? When designing or configuring a system for high availability, architects typically hope to offer some guarantee of uptime even in the presence of failure. Historically, it has been sufficient for the vast majority of systems to be available for less than 100 percent of the time, with some attempting to achieve the five nines, or 99.999, percent uptime.

The exact definition of high availability depends on the requirements of the application. This concept has gained increasing significance in the context of web applications, real-time systems, and other use cases that cannot afford any downtime. Database systems must not only guarantee system uptime, the ability to fulfill requests, but also ensure that the data itself remains available.

Traditionally, it has been difficult to make databases highly available, especially the relational database systems that have dominated the scene for the last couple of decades. These systems are most often designed to run on a single large machine, making it challenging to scale out to multiple machines.

Let's examine some of the reasons why many popular database systems have difficulty being deployed in high availability configurations, as this will allow us to have a greater understanding of the improvements that Cassandra offers. Exploring these reasons can help us to put aside previous assumptions that simply don't translate to the Cassandra model.

Therefore, in this chapter, we'll cover the following topics:

- The **Atomicity Consistency Isolation Durability (ACID)** properties
- Monolithic architecture
- Master-slave architecture, covering sharding and leader election
- Cassandra's approach to achieving high availability

Introducing the ACID properties

One of the most significant obstacles that prevents traditional databases from achieving high availability is that they attempt to strongly guarantee the ACID properties:

- **Atomicity**: This guarantees that database updates associated with a transaction occur in an all-or-nothing manner. If some part of the transaction fails, the state of the database remains unchanged.
- **Consistency**: This assures that the integrity of data will be preserved across all instances of that data. Changes to a value in one location will definitely be reflected in all other locations.
- **Isolation**: This attempts to ensure that concurrent transactions that manipulate the same data do so in a controlled manner, essentially isolating in-process changes from other clients. Most traditional relational database systems provide various levels of isolation with different guarantees at each level.
- **Durability**: This ensures that all writes are preserved in nonvolatile storage, most commonly on disk.

Database designers most commonly achieve these properties via write masters, locks, elaborate storage area networks, and the likeâ⊚⊚all of which tend to sacrifice availability. As a result, achieving some semblance of high availability frequently involves bolt-on components, log shipping, leader election, sharding, and other such strategies that attempt to preserve the original design.

Monolithic simplicity

The simplest design approach to guarantee ACID properties is to implement a monolithic architecture where all functions reside on a single machine. Since no coordination among nodes is required, the task of enforcing all the system rules is relatively straightforward.

Increasing availability in such architectures typically involves hardware layer improvements, such as RAID arrays, multiple network interfaces, and hot-swappable drives. However, the fact remains that even the most robust database server acts as a single point of failure. This means that if the server fails, the application becomes unavailable. This architecture can be illustrated with the following diagram:

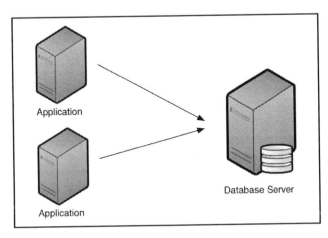

A common means of increasing capacity to handle requests on a monolithic architecture is to move the storage layer to a shared component such as a **storage area network (SAN)** or **network attached storage (NAS)**. Such devices are usually quite robust, with large numbers of disks and high-speed network interfaces. This approach is shown in a modification of the previous diagram, which depicts two database servers using a single NAS.

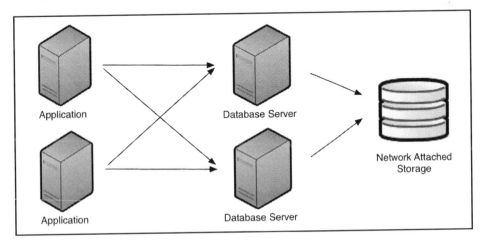

You'll notice that while this architecture increases the overall request-handling capacity of the system, it simply moves the single failure point from the database server to the storage layer. As a result, there is no real improvement from an availability perspective.

Scaling consistency – the master-slave model

As distributed systems have become more commonplace, the need for higher capacity distributed databases has grown. Many distributed databases still attempt to maintain ACID guarantees (or in some cases only the consistency aspect, which is the most difficult in a distributed environment), leading to the master-slave architecture.

In this approach, there might be many servers handling requests, but only one server can actually perform writes so as to maintain data in a consistent state. This avoids the scenario where the same data can be modified via concurrent mutation requests to different nodes. The following diagram shows the most basic scenario:

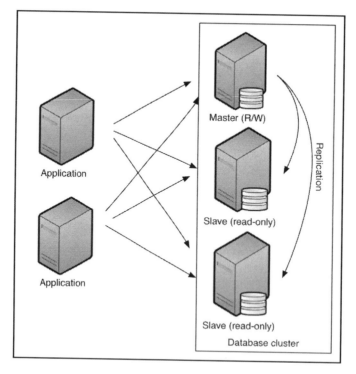

However, we still have not solved the availability problem, as a failure of the write master would lead to application downtime. It also means that writes do not scale well, since they are all directed to a single machine.

Using sharding to scale writes

A variation on the master-slave approach that enables higher write volumes is a technique called **sharding**, in which the data is partitioned into groups of keys, such that one or more masters can own a known set of keys. For example, a database of user profiles can be partitioned by the last name, such that **A-M** belongs to one cluster and **N-Z** belongs to another, as follows:

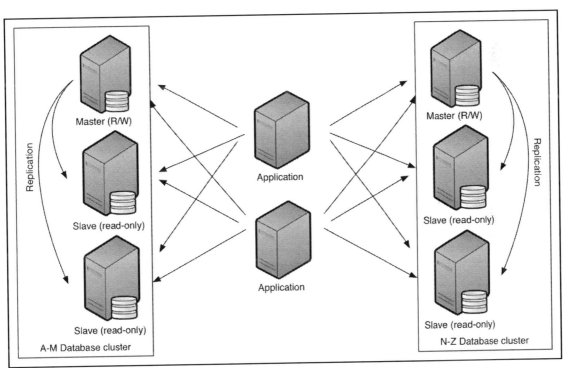

An astute observer will notice that both master-slave and sharding introduce failure points on the master nodes, and in fact the sharding approach introduces multiple points of failureâ©one for each master! Additionally, the knowledge of where requests for certain keys go rests with the application layer, and adding shards requires manual shuffling of data to accommodate the modified key ranges.

Some systems employ shard managers as a layer of abstraction between the application and the physical shards. This has the effect of removing the requirement that the application must have knowledge of the partition map. However, it does not obviate the need for shuffling data as the cluster grows.

Handling the death of the leader

A common means of increasing availability in the event of a failure on a master node is to employ a master failover protocol. The particular semantics of the protocol vary among implementations, but the general principle is that a new master is appointed when the previous one fails. Not all failover algorithms are equal; however, in general, this feature increases availability in a master-slave system.

Even a master-slave database that employs leader election suffers from a number of undesirable traits:

- Applications must understand the database topology
- Data partitions must be carefully planned
- Writes are difficult to scale
- A failover dramatically increases the complexity of the system in general, and especially so for multisite databases
- Adding capacity requires reshuffling data with a potential for downtime

Considering that our objective is a highly available system, and presuming that scalability is a concern, are there other options we need to consider?

Breaking with tradition – Cassandra's alternative

The reality is that not every transaction in every application requires full ACID guarantees, and ACID properties themselves can be viewed as more of a continuum where a given transaction might require different degrees of each property.

Cassandra's approach to availability takes this continuum into account. In contrast to its relational predecessorsâ and even most of its NoSQL contemporariesâ its original architects considered availability as a key design objective, with the intent to achieve the elusive goal of 100 percent uptime. Cassandra provides numerous knobs that give the user highly granular control of the ACID properties, all with different trade-offs.

The remainder of this chapter offers an introduction to Cassandra's high availability attributes and features, with the rest of the book devoted to help you to make use of these in real-world applications.

Cassandra's peer-to-peer approach

Unlike either monolithic or master-slave designs, Cassandra makes use of an entirely peer-to-peer architecture. All nodes in a Cassandra cluster can accept reads and writes, no matter where the data being written or requested actually belongs in the cluster. Internode communication takes place by means of a gossip protocol, which allows all nodes to quickly receive updates without the need for a master coordinator.

This is a powerful design, as it implies that the system itself is both inherently available and massively scalable. Consider the following diagram:

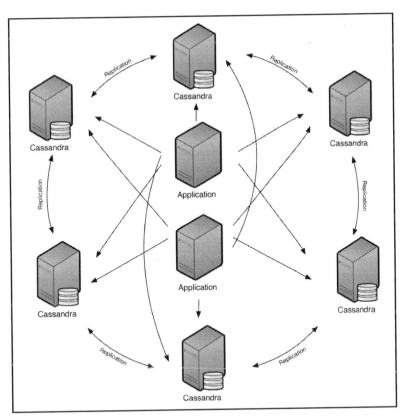

Note that in contrast to the monolithic and master-slave architectures, there are no special nodes. In fact, all nodes are essentially identical and as a result Cassandra has no single point of failure, and therefore no need for complex sharding or leader election. But how does Cassandra avoid sharding?

Hashing to the rescue

Cassandra is able to achieve both availability and scalability using a data structure that allows any node in the system to easily determine the location of a particular key in the cluster. This is accomplished by using a **distributed hash table** (**DHT**) design based on the Amazon Dynamo architecture.

As we saw in the previous diagram, Cassandra's topology is arranged in a ring, where each node owns a particular range of data. Keys are assigned to a specific node using a process called consistent hashing, which allows nodes to be added or removed without having to rehash every key based on the new range.

The node that owns a given key is determined by the chosen partitioner. Cassandra ships with several partitioner implementations, or developers can define their own by implementing a Java interface.

These topics will be covered in greater detail in the next chapter.

Replication across the cluster

One of the most important aspects of a distributed data store is the manner in which it handles replication of data across the cluster. If each partition were only stored on a single node, the system would effectively possess many single points of failure, and a failure of any node could result in catastrophic data loss. Such systems must therefore be able to replicate data across multiple nodes, making the occurrence of such loss less likely.

Cassandra has a sophisticated replication system, offering rack and data center awareness. This means it can be configured to place replicas in such a manner so as to maintain availability even during otherwise catastrophic events such as switch failures, network partitions, or data center outages. Cassandra also includes a mechanism that maintains the replication factor during node failures.

Replication across data centers

Perhaps the most unique feature Cassandra provides to achieve high availability is its multiple data center replication system. This system can be easily configured to replicate data across either physical or virtual data centers. This facilitates geographically dispersed data center placement without complex schemes to keep data in sync. It also allows you to create separate data centers for online transactions and heavy analysis workloads, while allowing data written in one data center to be immediately reflected in others.

Chapter 3, *Replication* and Chapter 4, *Data Centers*, will provide a complete discussion of Cassandra's extensive replication features.

The consistency continuum

Closely related to replication is the idea of consistency, the *C* in ACID that attempts to keep replicas in sync. Cassandra is often referred to as an eventually consistent system, a term that can cause fear and trembling for those who have spent many years relying on the strong consistency characteristics of their favorite relational databases. However, as previously discussed, consistency should be thought of as a continuum, not as an absolute.

With this in mind, Cassandra can be more accurately described as having tunable consistency, where the precise degree of consistency guarantee can be specified on a per-statement level. This gives the application architect ultimate control over the trade-offs between consistency, availability, and performance at the call level, rather than forcing a one-size-fits-all strategy onto every use case.

The CAP theorem

Any discussion of consistency would be incomplete without at least reviewing the CAP theorem. The CAP acronym refers to three desirable properties in a replicated system:

- **Consistency**: This means that the data should appear identical across all nodes in the cluster
- **Availability**: This means that the system should always be available to receive requests
- **Partition tolerance**: This means that the system should continue to function in the event of a partial failure

In 2000, computer scientist Eric Brewer from the University of California, Berkeley, posited that a replicated service can choose only two of the three properties for any given operation.

The CAP theorem has been widely misappropriated to suggest that entire systems must choose only two of the properties, which has led many to characterize databases as either AP or CP. In fact, most systems do not fit cleanly into either category, and Cassandra is no different.

Brewer himself addressed this misguided interpretation in his 2012 article, *CAP Twelve Years Later: How the "Rules" Have Changed*:

> ".. all three properties are more continuous than binary. Availability is obviously continuous from to 100 percent, but there are also many levels of consistency, and even partitions have nuances, including disagreement within the system about whether a partition exists"

In that same article, Brewer also pointed out that the definition of consistency in ACID terms differs from the CAP definition. In ACID, consistency refers to the guarantee that all database rules will be followed (unique constraints, foreign key constraints, and the like). The consistency in CAP, on the other hand, as clarified by Brewer, refers only to single-copy consistency, a strict subset of ACID consistency.

 When considering the various trade-offs of Cassandra's consistency level options, it's important to keep in mind that the CAP properties exist on a continuum rather than as binary choices.

The bottom line is that it's important to bear this continuum in mind when designing a system based on Cassandra. Refer to Chapter 3, *Replication*, for additional details on properly tuning Cassandra's consistency level under a variety of circumstances.

Summary

In this chapter we've discussed Cassandra's approach to availability and why the fundamental design decisions were made. The remainder of this book will build on this foundation. We will cover such topics as: how to configure Cassandra for high availability, design highly available applications on Cassandra, avoid common antipatterns, and handle various failure scenarios.

By the end of this book, you should possess a solid grasp of these concepts and be confident that you've successfully deployed one of the most robust and scalable database platforms available today.

However, we need to take it a step at a time, so in the next few chapters, we will build a deeper understanding of how Cassandra manages data. This foundation will be necessary for the topics covered later in the book. We'll start with a discussion of Cassandra's data placement strategy in the next chapter.

2
Data Distribution

Cassandra's peer-to-peer architecture and scalability characteristics are directly tied to its data placement scheme. Cassandra employs a **distributed hash table** data structure that allows for data to be stored and retrieved by key quickly and efficiently. **Consistent hashing** is at the core of this strategy, as it enables all nodes to understand where data exists in the cluster without complicated coordination mechanisms.

In this chapter, we'll cover the following topics:

- The fundamentals of distributed hash tables
- Cassandra's consistent hashing mechanism
- Token assignment, both manual and using vnodes
- The implications of Cassandra's partitioner implementations
- How hotspots form in the cluster

By the time you finish this chapter, you should have a deep understanding of these concepts. Let us begin with some basics about hash tables in general, and then we can delve deeper into Cassandra's distributed hash table implementation.

Hash table fundamentals

Most developers have experience with hash tables in some form, as nearly all programming languages include hash table implementations. Hash tables store data by applying a hash function to the object, which determines its placement in an underlying array.

While a detailed description of hashing algorithms is out of the scope of this book, it is sufficient for you to understand that a hash function simply maps any input data object (which may be any size) to some expected output. While the input may be large, the output of the hash function will be a fixed number of bits.

In a typical hash table design, the result of the hash function is divided by the number of array slots; the remainder then becomes the assigned slot number. Thus, the slot can be computed using **hash(o) % n**, where **o** is the object and **n** is the number of slots. Consider the following hash table, with names as keys and addresses as values:

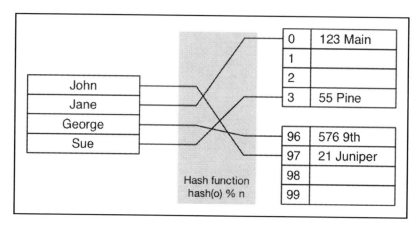

The values in the table on the left represent keys, which are then hashed using the hash function to produce the index of the slot where the value is stored.

In the preceding diagram, our input objects (**John**, **Jane**, **George**, and **Sue**), are put through the hash function, which results in an integer value. This value becomes the index in an array of street addresses. We can then look up the street address for a given name by computing its hash, then accessing the resulting array index.

This method works well when the number of slots is stable, or when the order of the elements can be managed in a predictable way by a single owner. There are additional complexities in hash table design, specifically around avoiding hash collisions, but the basic concept remains straightforward.

However, the situation gets a bit more complicated when multiple clients of the hash table need to stay in sync. These clients all need to consistently produce the same hash result even as the elements themselves may be moving around. Let's examine the distributed hash table architecture and the means by which it solves this problem.

Distributed hash tables

When we take the basic idea of a hash table and partition it out to multiple nodes, this is called a **distributed hash table (DHT)**. Each node in the DHT must share the same hash function, such that hash results on one node match all the others.

In order to determine the location of a given piece of data in the cluster, we need some means of associating an object with the node that owns it. We could ask every node in the cluster, but this would be problematic for at least two important reasons. First, this strategy doesn't scale well, as the overhead would grow with the number of nodes. Second, every node in the cluster would have to be available to answer requests in order to definitively state that a given item does not exist. A shared index could address this, but the result would be additional complexity and another point of failure.

Therefore, a key objective of the hash function in a DHT is to map a key to the node that owns it, such that a request can be made to the correct node. But the simple hash function discussed previously is no longer appropriate for mapping data to a node. The simple hash is problematic in a distributed system, because n translates to the number of nodes in the cluster and we know that n changes as nodes are added or removed. To illustrate this, we can modify our hash table to store pointers to machine IP addresses instead of street addresses:

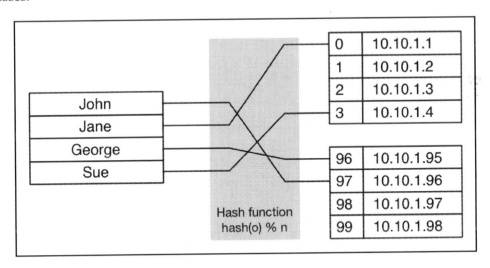

In this case, keys are mapped to a specific machine in the distributed hash table that holds the value for the key.

Now each key in the table can be mapped to its location in the cluster with a simple lookup. However, if we alter the cluster size (by adding or removing nodes), the result of the computation, and therefore the node mapping, changes for every object! Let's see what happens when a node is removed from the cluster:

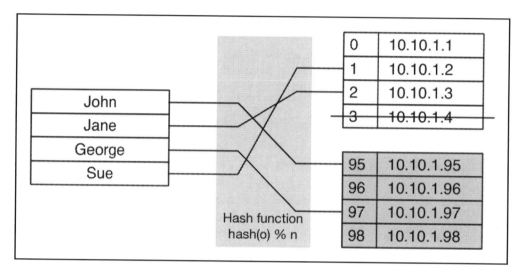

When a node is removed from the cluster, the result is that subsequent hash buckets are shifted, which causes the keys to point to different nodes.

Note that after removing node three, the number of buckets is reduced. As previously described, this changes the result of the hash function, causing the old mappings to become unusable. This would be catastrophic, as all key lookups would resolve to the wrong node.

Consistent hashing

The solution is consistent hashing. Introduced as a term in 1997, **consistent hashing** was originally used as a means of routing requests among a large number of web servers. It's easy to see how the web could benefit from a hash mechanism that allows any node in the network to efficiently determine the location of an object, in spite of the constant shifting of nodes in and out of the network. This is the fundamental objective of consistent hashing.

How it works

With consistent hashing, the buckets are arranged in a ring with a predefined range. The exact range depends on the partitioner being used. Keys are then hashed to produce a value that lies somewhere along the ring. Nodes are assigned a range, which is computed as follows:

Range start	Token value
Range end	Next token value *-1*

The following examples assume the default **Murmur3Partitioner** is used. For more information on this partitioner, take a look at the documentation, which can be found here: `http://docs.datastax.com/en/cassandra/3.x/cassandra/architecture/archPartitionerM3P.html`

Therefore, for a five-node cluster, a ring with evenly distributed token ranges would look like this, presuming the default Murmur3Partitioner is used:

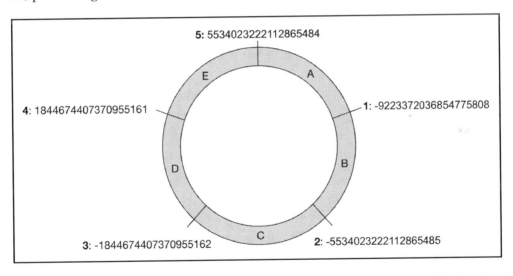

The primary replica for each key is assigned to a node based on its hashed value. Each node is responsible for the region of the ring between itself (inclusive) and its predecessor (exclusive).

This diagram represents data ranges (the letters) and the nodes (the numbers) that own those ranges. It may also be helpful to visualize this in table form, which may be more familiar to those who have used the `nodetool ring` command to view Cassandra's topology:

Node	Range Start	Range End
1	5534023222112865485	-9223372036854775808
2	-9223372036854775807	-5534023222112865485
3	-5534023222112865484	-1844674407370955162
4	-1844674407370955161	1844674407370955161
5	1844674407370955162	5534023222112865484

When Cassandra receives a key for either a read or a write, the same hash function is applied to the key to determine where it lies in the range. Since all nodes in the cluster are aware of the other nodes' ranges, any node can handle a request for any other node's range. The node receiving the request is called the **coordinator**, and any node can act in this role. If a key does not belong to the coordinator's range, it forwards the request to replicas in the correct range.

Following our previous example, we can now examine how our names might map to a hash, using the Murmur3 hash algorithm. Once the values are computed, they can be matched to the range of one of the nodes in the cluster, as follows:

Name	Hash value	Node assignment
John	-3916187946103363496	3
Jane	4290246218330003133	5
George	-7281444397324228783	2
Sue	-8489302296308032607	2

The placement of these keys might be easier to understand by visualizing their position in the ring:

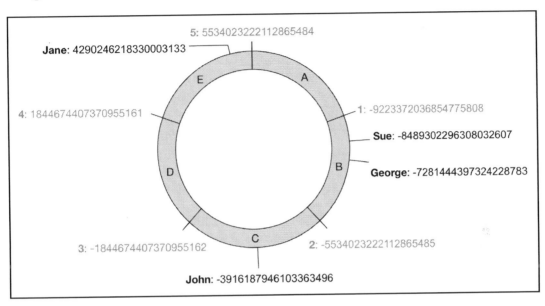

The hash value of the name keys determines their placement in the cluster

Now that you understand the basics of consistent hashing, let's turn our focus to the mechanism by which Cassandra assigns data ranges.

Token assignment

In Cassandra terminology, the start of the hash range is called a **token**, and until version 1.2, each node was assigned a single token, in the manner discussed in the previous section. Version 1.2 introduced the option to use virtual nodes, or vnodes as the feature is officially termed. Vnodes became the default option in the 2.0 release.

Cassandra determines where to place data by using the tokens assigned to each node. Nodes learn about these token assignments via gossip. Additional replicas are then placed based on the configured replication strategy and snitch. More details about replica placement can be found in Chapter 3, *Replication*.

Manually assigned tokens

If you have chosen not to use vnodes, you have the requirement to assign tokens manually. This is accomplished by setting the `initial_token` setting in `cassandra.yaml`.

Manual token assignment introduces a number of potential issues:

- **Adding and removing nodes**: When the size of the ring changes, all tokens must be recomputed and configuration files changed. This causes a significant amount of administrative overhead for a large cluster.
- **Node rebuilds**: In the case of a node rebuild, only a few nodes can participate in bootstrapping the replacement, leading to significant service degradation. We'll discuss this in detail later in this chapter.
- **Hot spots**: In some cases the relatively large range assigned to each node can cause hot spots if data is not evenly distributed.
- **Heterogeneous clusters**: With every node assigned a single token, the expectation is that all nodes will hold the same amount of data. Attempting to subdivide ranges to deal with nodes of varying sizes is a difficult and error-prone task.

Because of these issues, the use of vnodes is highly recommended for any new installation. For existing installations, migrating to vnodes will improve the performance, reliability, and administrative requirements of your cluster, especially during topology changes and failure scenarios.

> Use vnodes whenever possible to avoid issues with topology changes, node rebuilds, hot spots, and heterogeneous clusters.

If you must continue to manually assign tokens, make sure to set the correct value for `initial_token` any time nodes are added or removed. Failure to do so will almost always result in an unbalanced ring. If you have a Python interpreter, you can easily generate tokens with the following command (replacing `number_of_tokens` with the number of nodes in your cluster):

```
python -c 'print [str(((2**64 / number_of_tokens) * i) - 2**63) for i in
range(number_of_tokens)]'
```

For example, if you have a six-node cluster, you would issue this command:

```
python -c 'print [str(((2**64 / 6) * i) - 2**63) for i in range(6)]'
```

You can then use the values you generate as the `initial_token` settings for your nodes, with each node getting one of the values. It's best to always assign your tokens to the nodes in the same order to avoid unnecessary shuffling of data.

Vnodes

The concept behind vnodes is straightforward. Instead of a single token assigned to each node, it is now possible to specify the number of tokens using the `num_tokens` configuration property in `cassandra.yaml`. The default value is 256, which is sufficient for most use cases. A higher number generally results in better data distribution, while a lower number can lessen the time it takes to perform repairs and bootstrap operations. If you decide to use the default, making use of incremental repairs will help to offset this negative side effect.

When using vnodes, use `nodetool status` instead of `nodetool ring`, as the latter will output a row for every token across the cluster. Using `nodetool status` results in a much more readable output.

The following diagram illustrates a cluster without vnodes compared to one with vnodes enabled:

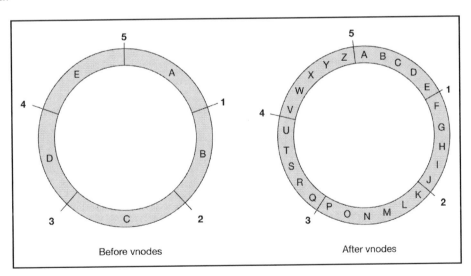

In this diagram, each numbered node is represented as a slice of the ring, where the tokens are represented as letters. Note that tokens are assigned randomly.

Remember that the letters represent ranges of data. You'll notice there are more ranges than nodes after enabling vnodes, and each node now owns multiple ranges.

How vnodes improve availability

While technically the cluster remains available during topology changes and node rebuilds, the level of degraded service has the potential to impact availability if the system remains under significant load. Vnodes offer a simple solution to the problems associated with manually assigned tokens. Let's examine the reasons why this is the case.

Adding and removing nodes

There are many reasons to change the size of a cluster. Perhaps you're increasing capacity for an anticipated growth in data or transaction volume, or maybe you're adding a data center for increased availability.

Considering that the objective is to handle greater load or provide additional redundancy, any significant performance degradation while adding or bootstrapping a new node is unacceptable as it counteracts these goals. Often in modern high-scale applications, slow is the same as unavailable. Equally important is to insure that new nodes receive a balanced share of the data.

Vnodes improve the bootstrapping process substantially:

- **More nodes can participate in data transfer**: Since the token ranges are more dispersed throughout the cluster, adding a new node involves ranges from a greater number of the existing nodes. As a result, machines involved in the transfer end up under less load than without vnodes, thus increasing the availability of those ranges.
- **Token assignment is automatic**: Cassandra handles the allocation of tokens, so there's no need to manually recalculate and reassign a new token for every node in the cluster. As a result, the ring becomes naturally balanced on its own.

Node rebuild

Rebuilding a node is a relatively common operation in a large cluster, as nodes will fail for a variety of reasons. Cassandra provides a mechanism for automatically rebuilding a failed node using replicated data.

When each node owns only a single token, that node's entire dataset is replicated to a number of nodes equal to the replication factor minus one. For example, with a replication factor of three, all the data on a given node will be replicated to two other nodes (replication will be covered in detail in `Chapter 3`, *Replication*). However, Cassandra will only use one replica in the rebuild operation.

So in this case, a rebuild operation involves three nodes, placing a high load on all three. Imagine that we have a six-node cluster, and **Node 2** has failed, requiring a rebuild. In the following diagram, note that each node only contains replicas for three tokens, preventing two of the nodes from participating in the rebuild:

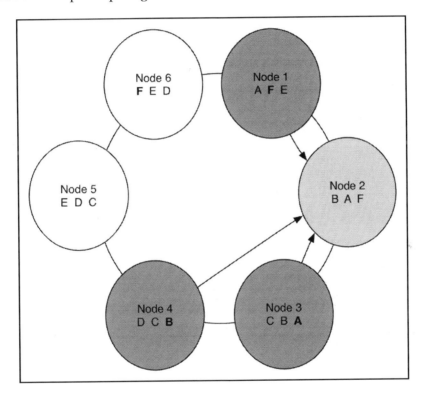

In the rebuilding of Node 2, only nodes 1, 3, and 4 can participate, because they contain the required replicas.

We can assume that reads and writes are continuing during this process. With one node down and three working hard to rebuild it, we now have only two out of six nodes operating at full capacity! Even worse, token ranges **A** and **B** reside entirely on nodes that are being taxed by this process, which can result in overburdening the entire cluster due to slow response times for those operations.

Vnodes provide significant benefits over manual token management for the rebuild process, as they distribute the load over many more nodes. This is the same concept as the benefit gained during the bootstrapping process. Since each node contains replicas for a larger (and random) variety of the available tokens, Cassandra can use these replicas in the rebuild process. Consider the following illustration of the same rebuild using vnodes:

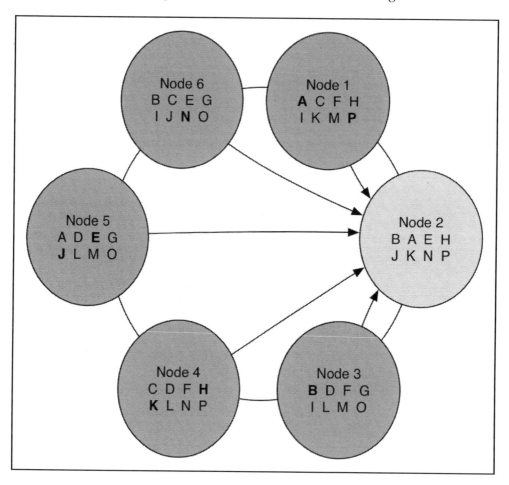

With vnodes, all nodes can participate in rebuilding node 2, because the tokens are spread more evenly across the cluster.

From the diagram you can see that rebuilding **Node 2** now involves the entire cluster, thus distributing the workload more evenly. This means each individual node is doing less work than without vnodes, resulting in greater operational stability.

Heterogeneous nodes

While it might be straightforward when initially building your Cassandra cluster to do so with nodes that are all identical, at some point older machines will need to be replaced with newer ones. This can create issues when manually assigning tokens, as it can become difficult to effectively choose the right tokens to produce a balanced result. This is especially problematic when adding or removing nodes, as it would become necessary to recompute the tokens to achieve a proper balance.

Vnodes ease this effort by allowing you to specify a *number* of tokens, instead of having to determine specific ranges. It is much easier to choose a proportionally larger number for newer, more powerful nodes than it is to determine proper token ranges. For example, if you have an existing cluster with *64* vnodes on each node, and you add nodes with twice the resources, you would want to increase the vnodes to *128* to compensate.

Partitioners

You may recall from the earlier discussion of distributed hash tables that keys are mapped to nodes via an implementation-specific hash function. In Cassandra's architecture, this function is determined by the partitioner you choose. This is a cluster-wide setting specified in `cassandra.yaml`. As of version 1.2, there are three options:

- **Murmur3Partitioner** (`org.apache.cassandra.dht.Murmur3Partitioner`): Produces an even distribution of data across the cluster using the Murmur3 hash algorithm. This is the default as of version 1.2, and should not be changed as it is measurably faster than the RandomPartitioner.
- **RandomPartitioner**(`org.apache.cassandra.dht.RandomPartitioner`): Similar to the Murmur3Partitioner, except that it computes an MD5 hash. This was the default prior to version 1.2.
- **ByteOrderedPartitioner** (`org.apache.cassandra.dht.ByteOrderedPartitioner`): Places keys in byte order (lexically) around the ring. This partitioner should generally be avoided for reasons explained in this section.

The only reason to switch from the default Murmur3Partitioner (to the ByteOrderedPartitioner) would be to enable range queries on keys (range queries on columns are always possible). However this decision must be carefully weighed, as there is a high likelihood that you'll end up with **hotspots**.

Hotspots

Let's assume, for example, that you're storing an address book, where the keys represent the surname of the contact. You want to use ByteOrderedPartitioner so you can search for all names between Smith and Watson. Using 2000 United States Census data as a guide, let's assume the distribution is as follows:

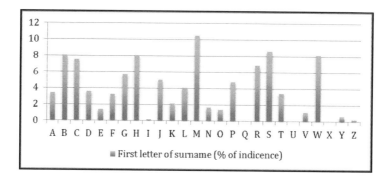

As one would expect, surnames in the United States are not evenly distributed by first letter. In fact, the distribution is quite uneven, and this imbalance translates directly to the data stored in Cassandra. If we presume that each node owns a subset of the keys alphabetically, the result would resemble the following:

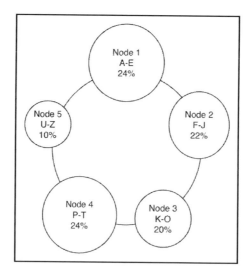

When using the ByteOrderedPartitioner, a table with surname as the key is likely to result in uneven data distribution.

The diagram clearly shows that the resulting distribution produces hotspots in **Node 1** and **Node 4**, while **Node 5** is significantly underutilized. One perhaps less obvious side effect of this imbalance is the impact on reads and writes. If we presume that both reads and writes follow the same distribution as the data itself (which is a logical assumption in this specific case), the heavier data nodes will also be required to handle more operations than the lighter data nodes.

A time-series example

Perhaps the most common use case for Cassandra is storing time-series data. Let's assume our use case involves writing log-style data, where we're always writing current timestamps and reading from relatively recent ranges of time. These are typical operations involved in time-series use cases, so it's natural to ask, *How can I query my data by date range?*

You'll recall that range queries on columns in Cassandra are possible using any partitioner, but only the ByteOrderedPartitioner allows for key-based range queries. Thus it's a common mistake to build a time-series model using time as a key and rely on ordering from BOP to perform range queries.

Let's assume a six-node cluster, where the key corresponds to time of day. If you are always writing current time, *your writes will always go to a single node!* Even worse, presuming you are reading recent ranges, your reads will *also* go to that same node. This diagram illustrates what happens when log data is being written, while the application is also requesting recent logs:

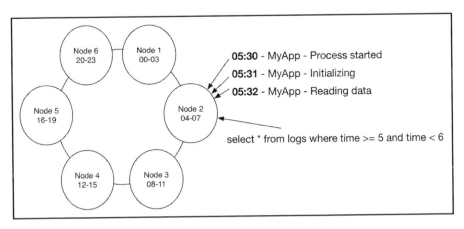

Time-series reads and writes using ByteOrderdPartitioner will concentrate on a small subset of nodes.

As you can see, **Node 2** is the only node doing any work. Each time the hour shifts, the workload will move to the next node in the ring. While the distribution of data in this model may be balanced (or it may not, depending on whether the application is busier at certain times), the workload will always experience hotspots.

We will discuss some more appropriate time-series data modeling techniques in detail in `Chapter 7`, *Modeling for Availability* . For now, consider it sufficient that you understand the implications of choosing the ByteOrderedPartitioner over one of the other options that uses a random hash function.

 In almost all cases the Murmur3Partitioner is the right choice. Use of the ByteOrderedPartitioner should be used with great caution, and can usually be avoided by altering the data model.

If you choose to use the ByteOrderedPartitioner, just remember that you will need to keep a close watch on your data distribution. Also you will have to ensure your reads and writes can be accomplished without overloading a subset of your nodes. In practice it's rarely necessary to store keys in order if you model your data correctly.

In `Chapter 7`, *Modeling for Availability* we'll discuss a number of data modeling strategies that can enable range queries without the drawbacks of the ByteOrderedPartitioner. For now, it's safe to assume that the Murmur3Partitioner is the safest choice, and this follows the recommendation made by Cassandra's core developers.

Summary

At this point, you should have a strong grasp of Cassandra's data distribution architecture, including consistent hashing, tokens, vnodes, and partitioners, as well as some of the causes of data hotspots. Your understanding of these fundamentals should help you to make sound design decisions that enable you to scale your cluster effectively and get the most out of your infrastructure investment.

In this chapter and the previous one, we've made reference a number of times to replication and its related concepts. In our next chapter, we'll discuss replication in depth, as replication is very important in determining the availability of data.

3
Replication

Replication is perhaps the most critical feature of a distributed data store, as it would otherwise be impossible to make any sort of availability guarantee in the face of a node failure. As you learned in `Chapter 1`, *Cassandra's Approach to High Availability*, Cassandra employs a sophisticated replication system that allows fine-grained control over replica placement and consistency guarantees.

In this chapter, we'll explore Cassandra's replication mechanism in depth, including the following topics:

- The replication factor
- How replicas are placed
- How Cassandra resolves consistency issues
- Maintaining the replication factor during node failures
- Consistency levels
- Choosing the right replication factor and consistency level

At the end of this chapter, you'll be able understand how to configure replication and tune consistency for your specific use cases. You'll be able to intelligently choose options that will provide the fault tolerance and consistency guarantees that are appropriate for your application.

Let's start with the basics: how Cassandra determines the number of replicas to be created and where to locate them in the cluster. We'll begin the discussion with a feature that you'll encounter the very first time you create a keyspace: *the replication factor*.

The replication factor

On the surface, setting the replication factor seems to be a fundamentally straightforward idea. You configure Cassandra with the number of replicas you want to maintain (during keyspace creation), and the system dutifully performs the replication for you, thus protecting you when something goes wrong. So by defining a replication factor of three, you will end up with a total of three copies of the data. There are a number of variables in this equation, and we'll cover many of these in detail in this chapter. Let's start with the basic mechanics of setting the replication factor.

Replication strategies

One thing you'll quickly notice is that the semantics to set the replication factor depend on the replication strategy you choose. The replication strategy tells Cassandra exactly how you want replicas to be placed in the cluster.

There are two strategies available:

- `SimpleStrategy`: This strategy is used for single data center deployments. It is fine to use this for testing, development, or simple clusters, but discouraged if you ever intend to expand to multiple data centers (including virtual data centers such as those used to separate analysis workloads).
- `NetworkTopologyStrategy`: This strategy is to be used when you have multiple data centers, or if you think you might have multiple data centers in the future. In other words, you should use this strategy for your production cluster.

SimpleStrategy

As a way of introducing this concept, we'll start with an example using `SimpleStrategy`. The following **Cassandra Query Language (CQL)** block will allow us to create a keyspace called `AddressBook` with three replicas:

```
CREATE KEYSPACE AddressBook
  WITH REPLICATION = {
    'class' : 'SimpleStrategy',
    'replication_factor' : 3
  };
```

You will recall from the previous chapter's section on token assignment that data is assigned to a node via a hash algorithm, resulting in each node owning a range of data. Let's take another look at the placement of our example data on the cluster. Remember the keys are first names, and we determined the hash using the Murmur3 hash algorithm.

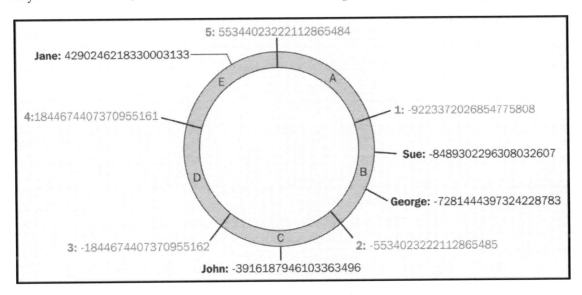

The primary replica for each key is assigned to a node based on its hashed value. Each node is responsible for the region of the ring between itself (inclusive) and its predecessor (exclusive).

While using `SimpleStrategy`, Cassandra will locate the first replica on the owner node (the one determined by the hash algorithm), then walk the ring in a clockwise direction to place each additional replica, as follows:

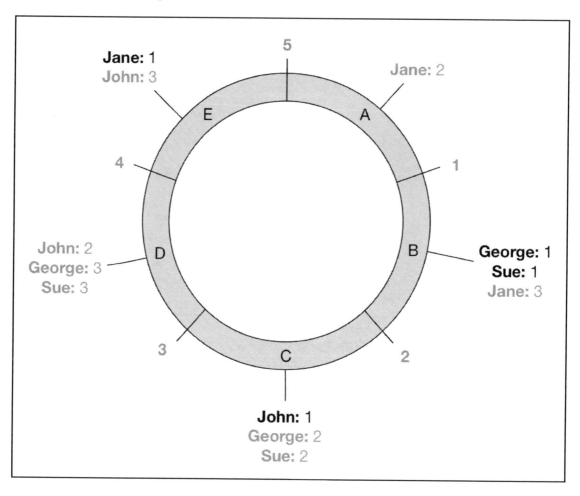

Additional replicas are placed in adjacent nodes when using manually assigned tokens

In the preceding diagram, the keys in bold represent the primary replicas (the ones placed on the owner nodes), with subsequent replicas placed in adjacent nodes, moving clockwise from the primary.

Although each node owns a set of keys based on its token range(s), there is no concept of a master replica. In Cassandra, unlike other database designs, every replica is equal. This means reads and writes can be made to any node that holds a replica of the requested key.

If you have a small cluster where all nodes reside in a single rack inside one data center, SimpleStrategy will do the job. This makes it the right choice for local installations, development clusters, and other similar simple environments where expansion is unlikely because there is no need to configure a snitch (which will be covered later in this section).

For production clusters, however, it is highly recommended that you use NetworkTopologyStrategy instead. This strategy provides a number of important features for more complex installations where availability and performance are paramount.

NetworkTopologyStrategy

When it's time to deploy your live cluster, NetworkTopologyStrategy offers two additional properties that make it more suitable for this purpose:

- **Rack awareness**: Unlike SimpleStrategy, which places replicas naively, this feature attempts to ensure that replicas are placed in different racks, thus preventing service interruption or data loss due to failures of switches, power, cooling, and other similar events that tend to affect single racks of machines.
- **Configurable snitches**: A snitch helps Cassandra to understand the topology of the cluster. There are a number of snitch options for any type of network configuration. We'll cover snitches in detail later in this chapter.

Here's a basic example of a keyspace using NetworkTopologyStrategy:

```
CREATE KEYSPACE AddressBook
  WITH REPLICATION = {
    'class' : 'NetworkTopologyStrategy',
    'dc1' : 3,
    'dc2' : 2
  };
```

In this example, we're telling Cassandra to place three replicas in a data center called dc1 and two replicas in a second data center called dc2. We'll spend more time discussing data centers in Chapter 4, *Data Centers*, but for now it is sufficient to point out that the data center names must match those configured in the snitch.

Snitches

As discussed earlier, Cassandra is able to intelligently place replicas across the cluster if you provide it with enough information about your topology. You give this insight to Cassandra through a snitch, which is set using the `endpoint_snitch` property in `cassandra.yaml`. The snitch is also used to help Cassandra route client requests to the closest nodes to reduce network latency.

As of version 2.0, there are eight available snitch options (and you can write your own as well):

- `SimpleSnitch`: This snitch is a companion to the `SimpleStrategy` replication strategy. It is designed for simple single data center configurations.
- `RackInferringSnitch`: As the name implies, this snitch attempts to infer your network topology. Using this snitch is discouraged because it assumes that your IP addressing scheme reflects your data center and rack configuration. For this to work properly, your addresses must be in the following form:

```
10 . 100 . 20 . 30
     data center   rack   node
```

- `PropertyFileSnitch`: Using this snitch allows the administrator to define which nodes belong in certain racks and data centers. You can configure this using `cassandra-topology.properties`. Each node in the cluster must be configured identically. You should generally prefer `GossipingPropertyFileSnitch`, because it handles the addition or removal of nodes without the need to update every node's `properties` file.
- `GossipingPropertyFileSnitch`: Unlike `PropertyFileSnitch`, where the entire topology must be defined on every node, this snitch allows you to configure each node with its own rack and data center, and then Cassandra gossips this information to the other nodes.
- `CloudstackSnitch`: This snitch sets data centers and racks using CloudStack's country, location, and availability zone.
- `GoogleCloudSnitch`: For Google Cloud deployments, this snitch automatically sets the region as the data center and the availability zone as the rack.

- **EC2Snitch**: This is similar to `GoogleCloudSnitch`, but for single-region EC2 deployments. This snitch also sets the region as the data center and the availability zone as the rack.
- **EC2MultiRegionSnitch**: This snitch assigns data centers and racks identically to `EC2Snitch`, with the difference being that it supports using public IP addresses for cross-data center communications.

> For production installations, it is almost always best to choose `GossipingPropertyFileSnitch` in physical data center environments and the appropriate cloud snitch in cloud environments.

Since much of the configuration related to snitches pertains to the topology of our data center, we will save our detailed treatment of this topic for `Chapter 4`, *Data Centers*, which will cover Cassandra's multiple data center features in detail.

Maintaining the replication factor when a node fails

One key way in which Cassandra maintains fault tolerance even during node failure is through a mechanism called **hinted handoff**. If you have set `hinted_handoff_enabled` to `true` in `cassandra.yaml` (which is the default), and one of the replica nodes is unreachable during a write, then the system will store a hint on the coordinator node (the node that receives the write). This hint contains the data itself along with information about where it belongs in the cluster. Hints are replayed to the replica node once the coordinator learns via gossip that the replica node is back online.

By default, Cassandra stores hints for up to 3 hours to avoid hint queues growing too long. This time window can be configured using the `max_hint_window_in_ms` property in `cassandra.yaml`. After this time period, it is necessary to run a repair to restore consistency. `Chapter 9`, *Failing Gracefully*, will include more in-depth coverage of hinted handoffs and how to ensure that your system recovers from longer node outages.

Now that we've covered the basics of replication, it's time to move on to the closely related topic of consistency. In most configurations, there will inevitably be occasions when not all replicas of a given bit of data are up to date. The specifics of how and when this occurs will be outlined later in this chapter. For now, let's find out how Cassandra handles those conflicts when they arise.

Consistency conflicts

In Chapter 1, *Cassandra's Approach to High Availability*, we discussed Cassandra's tunable consistency characteristics. For any given call, it is possible to achieve either strong consistency or eventual consistency. In the former case, we can know for certain that the copy of the data that Cassandra returns will be the latest. In the case of eventual consistency, the data returned may or may not be the latest, or there may be no data returned at all if the node is unaware of newly inserted data. Under eventual consistency, it is also possible to see deleted data if the node you're reading from has not yet received the delete request.

Depending on the read_repair_chance setting and the consistency level chosen for the read operation (more on this in the anti-entropy section later in this chapter), Cassandra might block the client and resolve the conflict immediately, or this might occur asynchronously. If data in conflict is never requested, the system will resolve the conflict the next time nodetool repair is run.

How does Cassandra know there is a conflict? Every column has three parts: key, value, and timestamp. Cassandra follows last-write-wins semantics, which means that the column with the latest timestamp always takes precedence.

Now, let's discuss one of the most important knobs a developer can turn to determine the consistency characteristics of their reads and writes.

Consistency levels

On every read and write operation, the caller must specify a consistency level, which lets Cassandra know what level of consistency to guarantee for that one call. The following table details the various consistency levels and their effects on both read and write operations:

Consistency level	Reads	Writes
ANY	This is not supported for reads.	Data must be written to at least one node, but permits writes via hinted handoff. Effectively allows a write to any node, even if all nodes containing the replica are down. A subsequent read might be impossible if all replica nodes are down.

ONE	The replica from the closest node will be returned.	Data must be written to at least one replica node (both commit log and memtable). Unlike ANY, hinted handoff writes are not sufficient.
TWO	The replicas from the two closest nodes will be returned.	The same as ONE, except two replicas must be written.
THREE	The replicas from the three closest nodes will be returned.	The same as ONE, except three replicas must be written.
QUORUM	Replicas from a quorum of nodes will be compared, and the replica with the latest timestamp will be returned.	Data must be written to a quorum of replica nodes (both commit log and memtable) in the entire cluster, including all data centers.
SERIAL	Permits reading uncommitted data as long as it represents the current state. Any uncommitted transactions will be committed as part of the read.	Similar to QUORUM, except that writes are conditional based on the support for lightweight transactions.
LOCAL_ONE	Similar to ONE, except that the read will be returned by the closest replica in the local data center.	Similar to ONE, except that the write must be acknowledged by at least one node in the local data center.
LOCAL_QUORUM	Similar to QUORUM, except that only replicas in the local data center are compared.	Similar to QUORUM, except the quorum must only be met using the local data center.
LOCAL_SERIAL	Similar to SERIAL, except only local replicas are used.	Similar to SERIAL, except only writes to local replicas must be acknowledged.
EACH_QUORUM	The opposite of LOCAL_QUORUM; requires each data center to produce a quorum of replicas, then returns the replica with the latest timestamp.	The opposite of LOCAL_QUORUM; requires a quorum of replicas to be written in each data center.
ALL	Replicas from all nodes in the entire cluster (including all data centers) will be compared, and the replica with the latest timestamp will be returned.	Data must be written to all replica nodes (both commit log and memtable) in the entire cluster, including all data centers.

As you can see, there are numerous combinations of read and write consistency levels, all with different ultimate consistency guarantees. To illustrate this point, let's assume that you would like to guarantee absolute consistency for all read operations. On the surface, it might seem as if you would have to read with a consistency level of ALL, thus sacrificing availability in the case of node failure.

But there are alternatives depending on your use case. There are actually two additional ways to achieve strong read consistency:

- **Write with consistency level of ALL**: This has the advantage of allowing the read operation to be performed using ONE, which lowers the latency for that operation. On the other hand, it means the write operation will result in UnavailableException if one of the replica nodes goes offline.
- **Read and write with QUORUM or LOCAL_QUORUM**: Since QUORUM and LOCAL_QUORUM both require a majority of nodes, using this level for both the write and the read will result in a full consistency guarantee (in the same data center when using LOCAL_QUORUM), while still maintaining availability during a node failure.

You should carefully consider each use case to determine what guarantees you actually require. For example, there might be cases where a lost write is acceptable, or occasions where a read need not be absolutely current. At times, it might be sufficient to write with a level of QUORUM, then read with ONE to achieve maximum read performance, knowing you might occasionally and temporarily return stale data. Cassandra gives you this flexibility, but it's up to you to determine how to best employ it for your specific data requirements. A good rule of thumb to attain strong consistency is that the read consistency level plus write consistency level should be greater than the replication factor.

 If you are unsure about which consistency levels to use for your specific use case, it's typically safe to start with LOCAL_QUORUM (or QUORUM for a single data center) reads and writes. This configuration offers strong consistency guarantees and good performance while allowing for the inevitable replica failure.

It is important to understand that even if you choose levels that provide less stringent consistency guarantees, Cassandra will still perform anti-entropy operations asynchronously in an attempt to keep replicas up to date.

Repairing data

Cassandra employs a multifaceted anti-entropy mechanism that keeps replicas in sync. Data repair operations generally fall into three categories:

- **Synchronous read repair**: When a read operation requires comparing multiple replicas, Cassandra will initially request a checksum from the other nodes. If the checksum doesn't match, the full replica is sent and compared with the local version. The replica with the latest timestamp will be returned and the old replica will be updated. This means that in normal operations, old data is repaired when it is requested.
- **Asynchronous read repair**: Each table in Cassandra has a setting called `read_repair_chance` (as well as its related setting, `dclocal_read_repair_chance`), which determines how the system treats replicas that are not compared during a read. The default setting of `0.1` means that 10 percent of the time, Cassandra will also repair the remaining replicas during read operations.
- **Manually running repair**: A full repair (using `nodetool repair`) should be run regularly to clean up any data that has been missed as part of the previous two operations. At a minimum, it should be run once every `gc_grace_seconds`, which is set in the table schema and defaults to 10 days.

One might ask what the consequence would be of failing to run a repair operation within the window specified by `gc_grace_seconds`. The answer relates to Cassandra's mechanism to handle deletes. As you might be aware, all modifications (or mutations) are immutable, so a delete is really just a marker telling the system not to return that record to any clients. This marker is called a **tombstone**.

Cassandra performs garbage collection on data marked by a tombstone each time a compaction occurs. If you don't run the repair, you risk deleted data reappearing unexpectedly. In general, deletes should be avoided when possible as the unfettered buildup of tombstones can cause significant issues. For more information on this topic, refer to `Chapter 8`, *Anti-Patterns*.

In the course of normal operations, Cassandra will repair old replicas when their records are requested. Thus, it can be said that read repair operations are lazy, such that they only occur when required.

With all these options for replication and consistency, it can seem daunting to choose the right combination for a given use case. Let's take a closer look at this balance to help bring some additional clarity to the topic.

Balancing the replication factor with consistency

There are many considerations when choosing a replication factor, including availability, performance, and consistency. Since our topic is high availability, let's presume your desire is to maintain data availability in the case of node failure.

It's important to understand exactly what your failure tolerance is, and this will likely be different depending on the nature of the data. The definition of failure is probably going to vary among use cases as well, as one case might consider data loss a failure, whereas another accepts data loss as long as all queries return.

Achieving the desired availability, consistency, and performance targets requires coordinating your replication factor with your application's consistency level configurations. In order to assist you in your efforts to achieve this balance, let's consider a single data center cluster of 10 nodes and examine the impact of various configuration combinations, **replication factor(RF)**:

RF	Write CL	Read CL	Consistency	Availability	Use cases
1	ONE QUORUM ALL	ONE QUORUM ALL	Consistent	Doesn't tolerate any replica loss	Data can be lost and availability is not critical, such as analysis clusters
2	ONE	ONE	Eventual	Tolerates loss of one replica	Maximum read performance and low write latencies are required, and sometimes returning stale data is acceptable
2	QUORUM ALL	ONE	Consistent	Tolerates loss of one replica on reads, but none on writes	Read-heavy workloads where some downtime for data ingest is acceptable (improves read latencies)

2	ONE	QUORUM ALL	Consistent	Tolerates loss of one replica on writes, but none on reads	Write-heavy workloads where read consistency is more important than availability
3	ONE	ONE	Eventual	Tolerates loss of two replicas	Maximum read and write performance are required, and sometimes returning stale data is acceptable
3	QUORUM	ONE	Eventual	Tolerates loss of one replica on write and two on reads	Read throughput and availability are paramount, while write performance is less important, and sometimes returning stale data is acceptable
3	ONE	QUORUM	Eventual	Tolerates loss of two replicas on write and one on reads	Low write latencies and availability are paramount, while read performance is less important, and sometimes returning stale data is acceptable
3	QUORUM	QUORUM	Consistent	Tolerates loss of one replica	Consistency is paramount, while striking a balance between availability and read/write performance
3	ALL	ONE	Consistent	Tolerates loss of two replicas on reads, but none on writes	Additional fault tolerance and consistency on reads is paramount at the expense of write performance and availability
3	ONE	ALL	Consistent	Tolerates loss of two replicas on writes, but none on reads	Low write latencies and availability are paramount, but read consistency must be guaranteed at the expense of performance and availability
3	ANY	ONE	Eventual	Tolerates loss of all replicas on write and two on read	Maximum write and read performance and availability are paramount, and often returning stale data is acceptable (note that hinted writes are less reliable than the guarantees offered at **CL ONE**)

3	ANY	QUORUM	Eventual	Tolerates loss of all replicas on write and one on read	Maximum write performance and availability are paramount, and sometimes returning stale data is acceptable
3	ANY	ALL	Consistent	Tolerates loss of all replicas on writes, but none on reads	Write throughput and availability are paramount, and clients must all see the same data, even though they might not see all writes immediately

There are also two additional consistency levels, SERIAL and LOCAL_SERIAL, which can be used to read the latest value, even if it is part of an uncommitted transaction. Otherwise, they follow the semantics of QUORUM and LOCAL_QUORUM, respectively.

As you can see, there are numerous possibilities to consider when choosing these values, especially in a scenario involving multiple data centers. This discussion will give you greater confidence as you design your applications to achieve the desired balance.

Summary

In this chapter, we introduced the foundational concepts of replication and consistency. In our discussion, we outlined the importance of the relationship between replication factor and consistency level, and their impact on performance, data consistency, and availability.

By now, you should be able to make sound decisions specific to your use cases. This chapter might serve as a handy reference in the future, as it can be challenging to keep all these details in mind.

In the previous two chapters, we've been gradually expanding from how Cassandra locates individual pieces of data to its strategy to replicate it and keep it consistent.

In the next chapter, we'll take things a step further and take a look at its multiple data center capabilities, as no highly available system is truly complete without the ability to distribute itself geographically.

4

Data Centers

One of Cassandra's most compelling high availability features is its support for multiple data centers. In fact, this feature gives it the capability to scale reliably with a level of ease that few other data stores can match.

In this chapter, we'll explore Cassandra's data center support, covering the following topics:

- Use cases for multiple data centers
- Using a separate data center for online analytics
- Replication across data centers
- An in-depth look at configuring snitches
- Multi-region EC2 implementations
- Multi-data center consistency levels

Database administrators have struggled for many years to reliably replicate data across multiple geographies, a task that is made especially difficult when that system is attempting to maintain ACID guarantees. The best we could typically hope for was to keep a relatively recent backup for failover purposes.

Distributed database designs have made this easier, but many still require complex configurations and have significant limitations when replicating across data centers. Cassandra allows you to maintain a complete set of replicas in more than one data center with relative ease. Let's start by examining some of the reasons why users may want to deploy multiple data centers.

As we look at each option, think about your own use cases and into which category they may fall. Doing so will help you to make the right deployment decisions to make the best use of your Cassandra investment.

Use cases for multiple data centers

There are several key use cases for deploying Cassandra across multiple data centers, including the obvious failover and load balancing scenarios. Let's examine a few of these cases.

Live backup

Traditional database backups involve taking periodic snapshots of the data and storing them offsite in case the system fails, in which case there will be downtime as a new system is brought up and the data is restored. This strategy also inevitably leads to data loss for the time period between the last backup and the point of failure.

Cassandra supports these types of backups, and we will discuss this in greater depth in Chapter 9, *Failing Gracefully*. While snapshot backups are still useful to protect against data corruption or accidental updates, Cassandra's data center support can be used to provide a current backup for cases such as hardware failures.

The basic idea involves setting up a second data center that maintains a current set of replicas that can be used to rebuild the primary cluster, should a catastrophic event cause the loss of an entire data center.

For this use case, it is typically sufficient to maintain a smaller cluster with a replication factor of one, as the system will never be used to accept live reads or writes. The primary consideration in this case is storage capacity to handle the same quantity of data as the live data center.

Failover

The failover scenario is very similar to the backup use case we just discussed, except that the backup data center is generally allocated similar resources as the primary cluster. Additionally, while a single replica may suffice for a backup data center, generally speaking a failover data center should be configured with the same replication factor as the primary, since it may take over responsibility for the full application load in the event of a failure.

It's also important to consider whether you expect your failover data center to handle a full production load. Presuming this is the case, you will need to ensure it has adequate capacity to handle this. Having a hot failover data center protects you from a common single point of failure: the power supply to your hosts. In EC2 you can choose to configure your hosts to run in multiple availability zones, as each is supplied with a separate power source. If you do this while using the **EC2 snitch**, be sure to allocate your nodes evenly across zones, as the snitch will place replicas across multiple zones. Failure to do this can lead to hot spots.

 It would be ill-advised to assume you can maintain a small failover data center, and then simply add multiple nodes in the case of failure. The additional overhead of bootstrapping the new nodes would actually reduce capacity at a critical point when the capacity is needed most.

Load balancing

In some cases applications may be configured to route traffic to any node in the cluster, without taking into account a specific data center. This has the effect of load balancing the requests across multiple data centers, and can be useful in cases where the data centers share a high-bandwidth connection.

In this instance, the objective is to provide redundancy, so each data center must be able to handle the entire application load, similarly to the failover scenario. However, there are a couple of important considerations when taking this approach:

- Absolute consistency is expensive to guarantee in this scenario, because doing so typically requires replicating the data across higher latency connections. If strong consistency is paramount for your use case, you should consider employing a geographic distribution model as described in the next section.
- This usage pattern is most appropriate for use cases where eventual consistency is acceptable, such as event capture, time-series data, logging, and so on, where the primary read case involves offline data analysis rather than real-time queries.

Geographic distribution

Often application architects will find it necessary for latency reasons to send requests to a data center located near the originator, or to mitigate the potential impact of natural disasters. This is particularly useful for systems that span the globe, where routing all requests to a central location is impractical. The ability to locate data centers in strategic global locations around the world can be an indispensable feature in these scenarios.

This approach is often desirable for applications where both performance and strong consistency are important. The reason for this is that clients are guaranteed to make requests to a single data center, enabling the use of the LOCAL_QUORUM consistency level, which means they won't suffer a performance penalty by waiting for a remote data center to acknowledge the write. The following diagram illustrates this configuration:

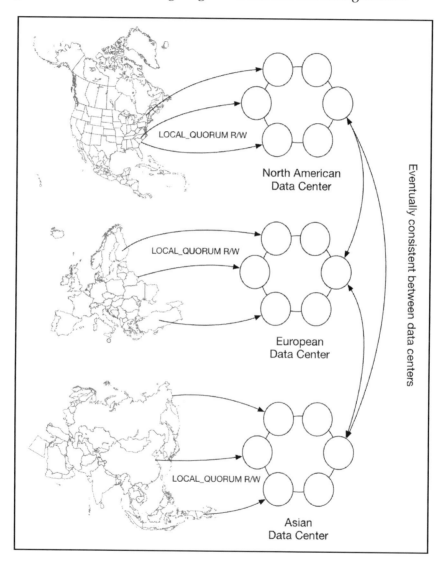

In this scenario, the idea is that clients should detect the failure of a data center and fall back to one of the others. There is the possibility of reading old data if it was written with a local consistency level, but in many cases, stale data is better than application down time. This can be visualized as follows:

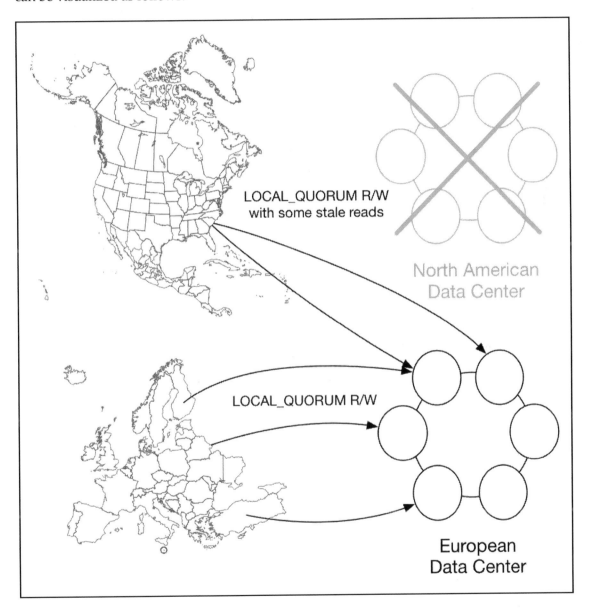

In this scenario, the **North American Data Center** experiences a failure, which requires clients in North America to redirect to the **European Data Center** during the outage. Obviously, the **European Data Center** must have sufficient capacity to handle the additional load.

It's important to make sure your application is capable of handling this scenario, as the latency will increase and reads may produce some stale data. A good strategy is to limit the interaction with the database to only those operations that are critical to the continued functioning of the application.

Online analysis

So far we've discussed use cases that may be obvious to experienced database users. But Cassandra supports an additional scenario that is particularly useful in the context of a NoSQL database that doesn't provide a built-in ad hoc query mechanism. The use of a data center for analysis purposes has become commonplace among Cassandra users, as it provides the benefits of a scalable NoSQL solution with the power of modern data analysis tools.

Traditional data analysis (referred to as **Online Analytical Processing(OLAP)**), typically involves taking normalized data from the transactional relational database and moving it into a denormalized form for faster analysis. This process involves significant **Extract, Transform and Load** (ETL) overhead, which inherently results in a delay in analyzing the data.

Cassandra's support for multiple data centers, in combination with its robust integrations with the Hadoop and Spark frameworks, allows users to conduct sophisticated batch or real-time analysis using live data with no ETL overhead. This is accomplished by dedicating a separate data center for analysis then isolating this data center from live traffic.

For many use cases a single replica is sufficient for an analysis data center, as short periods of downtime are frequently acceptable for batch analysis purposes. However, if you require 100% uptime for your analysis workloads, you may need to specify a higher replication factor. Additional replicas also means the analysis data center is less likely to drop writes, especially while heavy analysis jobs are running. Also, make sure to run repairs regularly to keep data consistent.

There are currently two popular open source analysis projects with excellent Cassandra integration:

- **Hadoop**: Cassandra has included support for Hadoop since the very early revisions, and the DataStax Enterprise offering even provides a replacement for **Hadoop Distributed File System (HDFS)** called **CassandraFS**. Having said that, while Hadoop was quite revolutionary at its introduction, it is beginning to show its age.
- **Spark**: The Spark project has gained significant traction in a very short amount of time as a primarily in-memory replacement for Hadoop. The excellent open source integration with Cassandra, supported by DataStax, allows much faster and more elegant analysis work to be performed against native Cassandra data. If you don't already have a significant Hadoop investment, the Spark integration is most likely the better choice.

Regardless of which path you choose, it's important to realize that the old OLAP paradigms no longer apply.

The key to successfully processing large amounts of distributed data is to bring the processing to the data, rather than the data to the processing. This was the key innovation with MapReduce.

In the new world of large datasets, shipping data across the network using complex ETL processes is no longer a viable solution. We must co-locate the processing framework with the database. Let's explore how to do this using both Hadoop and Spark.

Analysis using Hadoop

Hadoop is actually an ecosystem comprised of multiple projects, a full discussion of which would be too much for this chapter. For our purposes, we will simply point out the important processes and how they should be deployed with Cassandra.

Under the covers, Hadoop makes extensive use of HDFS to write temporary data to disk. HDFS components include the **NameNode** and **2ndaryNameNode** (which live on a master node), and **DataNode** (which hold the data itself). If you use DataStax Enterprise, these components are replaced by CassandraFS, which uses Cassandra as the underlying filesystem.

The actual analysis work is performed by the MapReduce framework, which consists of a global **ResourceManager** and one **ApplicationManager** for each application (which run on the master) and **NodeManager** (which is co-located with the **DataNode).**

The canonical Cassandra-Hadoop integration places DataNodes and NodeManagers on each Cassandra node in the analysis data center. This allows the data owned by each node to be processed locally rather than having to be retrieved from across the network. This idea is fundamental to the ability to process large amounts of data in an efficient manner. In fact, shuffling data across the network is typically the most significant time sink in any analysis work. The following diagram shows how this configuration looks:

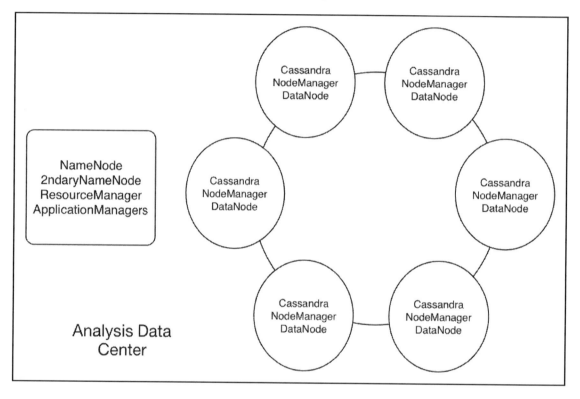

The canonical Hadoop-Cassandra topology involves co-locating NodeManagers and DataNodes with the Cassandra instances.

It is tempting, if you have an existing Hadoop installation, to try to move data from Cassandra into that cluster. However, a better strategy is to install Cassandra on that cluster. Alternatively, you can use a separate cluster to process your Cassandra data, and then move the results into your existing cluster.

In any case, it is worth considering migrating to Spark, as it is a much more modern attempt at distributed data processing.

Analysis using Spark

To use Spark for analyzing Cassandra data, you will essentially be replacing the MapReduce component of your Hadoop installation with the Spark processes. The Spark Master process replaces the ResourceManager and ApplicationManager, and the Worker processes take over the job of the NodeManagers, as follows:

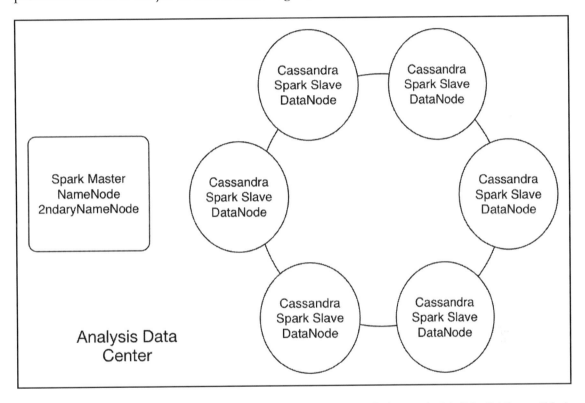

Running Spark with Cassandra involves replacing the Hadoop ResourceManager and ApplicationManagers with a Spark master, and replacing Hadoop NodeManagers with Spark Slaves.

While Spark appears to be rapidly gaining traction in the analysis space, many of the existing tools and frameworks are built around Hadoop and MapReduce. Additionally, a large number of users have existing investments in the Hadoop ecosystem, making a wholesale move to Spark impractical.

The good news is the two can live together in harmony. In fact, you can simply add Spark processes to your existing infrastructure, provided that you have sufficient resources to do so. You can also employ two analysis data centers, one for Hadoop jobs and one for Spark jobs. Cassandra offers tremendous flexibility here.

Now that we've covered the basic scenarios where multiple data centers prove useful, let's take a deep dive into data center configuration.

Data center setup

The mechanism for defining a data center depends on the snitch you specify in `cassandra.yaml`. Take a look at the previous chapter if you need a refresher on the various types of snitches. You'll recall that the snitch's role is to tell Cassandra what your network topology looks like, so it can know how to place replicas across your cluster. When configuring a snitch, it's important to make sure that the data centers resolved by the snitch match those in your schema.

With this in mind, let's take a closer look at what configuration looks like for each of the snitch options.

RackInferringSnitch

There really isn't any configuration to perform on the `RackInferringSnitch`, as long as your IP addressing scheme matches your topology. Specifically, it uses the second, third, and fourth octets to define data center, rack, and node, respectively, as follows:

```
10 . 100 . 20 . 30
     data center  rack  node
```

This strategy can work well for simple deployments in physical data centers where IP addresses can be predicted reliably. The problem is that this rarely works out well over the long term, as network requirements often change over time, and ensuring all network administrators abide by these rules can be difficult. In general, it's better to use one of the other more explicit snitches.

As a general rule, it is preferable to deploy a single rack configuration in each data center, as opposed to using the rack awareness feature. This applies to any snitch that allows specifying racks. While the initial configuration may be straightforward, it can be difficult to scale the multiple rack strategy. Rack configurations have a tendency to change over time, and often the people who manage the hardware are not the same people who handle Cassandra configuration. In this case, simplicity is often the best strategy.

PropertyFileSnitch

The `PropertyFileSnitch` allows an administrator to precisely configure the topology of the network by means of a properties file named `cassandra-topology.properties`. The following is an example configuration, representing a cluster with three data centers, where the first two have two racks each, and the analysis cluster has a single rack:

```
# US East Data Center
50.11.22.33 =DC1:RAC1
50.11.22.44 =DC1:RAC1
50.11.22.55 =DC1:RAC1
50.11.33.33 =DC1:RAC2
50.11.33.44 =DC1:RAC2
50.11.33.55 =DC1:RAC2

# US West Data Center
172.11.22.33 =DC2:RAC1
172.11.22.44 =DC2:RAC1
172.11.22.55 =DC2:RAC1
172.11.33.33 =DC2:RAC2
172.11.33.44 =DC2:RAC2
172.11.33.55 =DC2:RAC2

# Analysis Cluster
172.11.44.11 =DC3:RAC1
172.11.44.22 =DC3:RAC1
172.11.44.33 =DC3:RAC1

# Default for unspecified nodes
default =DC3:RAC1
```

This diagram shows what this cluster would look like visually:

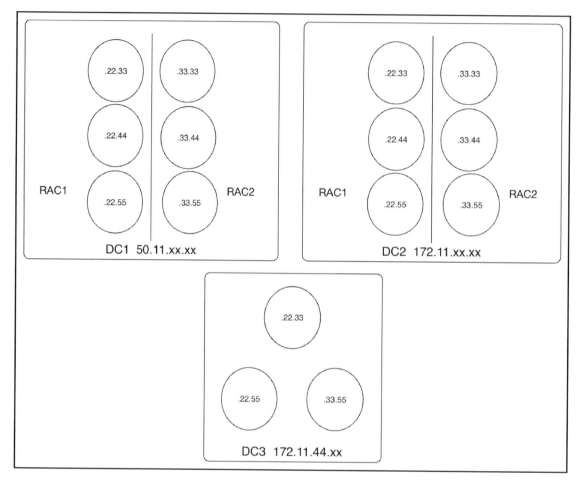

This is a visual representation of the sample PropertyFileSnitch configuration.

This example demonstrates a cluster with two physical data centers and one virtual data center used for analysis. It is worth noting that in the specific case above, the RackInferringSnitch would automatically choose essentially the same topology, since the IP addresses conform to its required scheme.

GossipingPropertyFileSnitch

One of the principal challenges when using the `PropertyFileSnitch` is that the configuration file must be kept in sync on all nodes. This can be difficult, as the file is reloaded automatically without restarting. While modern cluster management tools certainly ease this burden, the `GossipingPropertyFileSnitch` solves the problem completely.

Rather than using `cassandra-topology.properties`, you specify the data center and rack membership for each node in its own configuration file. In each node's `$CASSANDRA_HOME/conf` directory, you'll need to place a file called `cassandra-rackdc.properties`, which should conform to the following example:

```
dc =DC1
rack =RAC1
# Uncomment the following line to make this snitch prefer the internal ip
when possible, as the Ec2MultiRegionSnitch does.
# prefer_local=true
```

Once this file is in place (and the `GossipingPropertyFileSnitch` is selected in `cassandra.yaml`), as the name implies, Cassandra will gossip the data center and rack information to the other nodes in the cluster. Remember that Cassandra is a peer-to-peer system, and the gossip mechanism allows a Cassandra node to communicate state changes with nearby peers. This eliminates the need for a centralized configuration, and in general, better conforms to the principles behind Cassandra's peer-to-peer architecture.

So far we've examined snitches that work well when you control the network configuration on your nodes, as is the case with physical, non-cloud data centers. With the proliferation of cloud deployments on Amazon's EC2 infrastructure, this is not always the case.

Cloud snitches

Amazon EC2, Google Cloud, and CloudStack can be excellent places to run Cassandra, as much work has been put into getting it right. This section will focus on EC2 deployments, as they are the most common at the time of writing. But the general principles apply to all the cloud snitches.

If you're planning on going this route, be sure to check out the plethora of fantastic open source tools available from Netflix, who have put significant time and energy into perfecting the art of deploying and running Cassandra on EC2. Their engineering blog also has loads of great content that's worth a look.

This book will avoid making any recommendations for specific instance types or configurations, as requirements are unique for different use cases. However, the one exception is that running on ephemeral SSDs is highly recommended, as you will see tremendous performance gains from doing so.

When it comes to configuring Cassandra on EC2, the `EC2MultiRegionSnitch` will come in handy. If you already manage deployments on EC2 you'll be aware of the frequently transient nature of its network configurations. This snitch is designed to ease the burden of managing this often troublesome issue.

When using the `EC2MultiRegionSnitch`, data center and rack configuration becomes tied directly to region and availability zone, respectively. Thus, a node in region us-east, availability zone 1a, will be assigned to a data center named `us-east` and a rack named `1a`.

Additionally, since many deployments involve virtual data centers that are logically separated but located in the same physical region, this snitch allows us to specify a suffix to be applied to the data center name. This involves setting the `dc_suffix` property in `cassandra-rackdc.properties`, as follows:

```
dc_suffix=_live
```

With this suffix in place, the data center will now be named `us-east_live`.

 When deploying Cassandra in EC2 with the multi-region snitch, make sure to set your `broadcast_address` to the external IP address, and your `rpc_address` and `listen_address` should be set to the internal IP address. These values can be found in `cassandra.yaml`. This will allow your nodes to communicate across data centers while keeping your client traffic local to the data center in which it resides.

In order to achieve the greatest amount of protection from failures in EC2, it is advisable to deploy your nodes across multiple availability zones in each region. Amazon's availability zones operate as isolated locations with high bandwidth network configurations between them, and Cassandra's rack awareness features can guarantee replica placement in multiple zones. Keep in mind that you need to evenly distribute nodes across availability zones to achieve even replica distribution.

The following diagram shows an example of an optimal configuration, with data centers in two regions in addition to an analysis cluster. This is similar to the diagram shown previously using the `PropertyFileSnitch`.

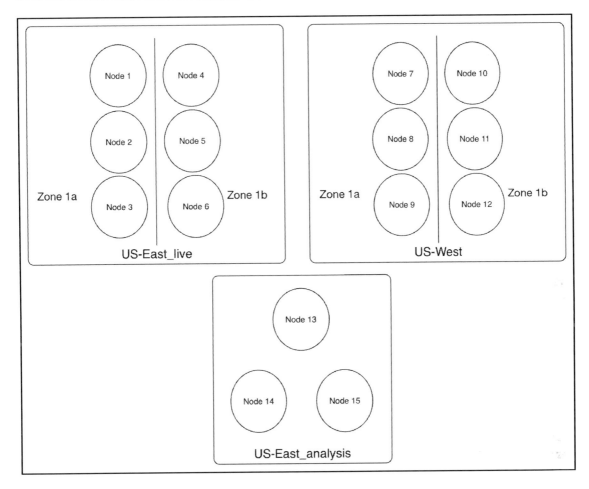

When using a cloud snitch, data centers correlate to regions while racks are assigned based on availability zones.

This topology mirrors the previous example, except the naming convention follows AWS regions and availability zones. In the US-East data center, the `dc_suffix` is defined as `"_live"` for the nodes that accept live traffic, and `"_analysis"` for the nodes isolated for read-heavy analytic workloads.

You should now have a good understanding of how to configure your cluster for multiple data centers. Let us now explore how Cassandra replicates data across these data centers, and how multiple data centers influence the balance between consistency, availability, and performance.

Replication across data centers

In previous chapters, we have touched on the idea that Cassandra can automatically replicate across multiple data centers. There are other systems that allow for similar replication; however, the ease of configuration and general robustness set Cassandra apart. Let's take a detailed look at how this works.

Setting replication factors

You will recall from Chapter 3, *Replication* that replication is configured via CQL at the keyspace level. Since we're on the topic of multiple data centers, it's important to understand that you'll always want to use the NetworkTopologyStrategy, since the SimpleStrategy does not allow for setting replication factor for each data center.

Attempting to use SimpleStrategy in a multi-data center environment would result in random replica placement across data centers. Coordination traffic across nodes would incur significant latency, as requests would often require nodes in more than one data center to satisfy the requested consistency level.

Using our example physical topology from the earlier PropertyFileSnitch section, the following statement will create a keyspace, users, with three replicas in each of our two live data centers, as well as one in the analysis data center:

```
CREATE KEYSPACE users
  WITH REPLICATION = {
    'class' : 'NetworkTopologyStrategy',
    'DC1' : 3,
    'DC2' : 3,
    'DC3' : 1
  }
```

Now each column in the database will have seven total replicas, dispersed across five distinct racks in two different data centers, without any complex configuration.

Consistency in a multiple data center environment

In this section, we will take a look at how Cassandra moves data from one data center to another. It is easy to understand the concept of replication in a local context, but it may seem more difficult to grasp the idea that Cassandra can seamlessly transfer large amounts of data across high-latency connections in real time.

As you may now suspect, the precise replication behavior depends on your chosen consistency level. In the last chapter, we explored each consistency level in detail, as well as its impact on availability, consistency, and performance.

In a multiple data center environment, it is extremely important to remember that using a non-local consistency level (ALL, ONE, TWO, THREE, QUORUM, SERIAL, or EACH_QUORUM) may have an impact on performance. This is because these consistency levels do not always route requests to the local data center; they will prefer local nodes in the sense that they sort based on the snitch, but there is no locality guarantee. If you do this, you will end up with a scenario that resembles this diagram (assuming there are clients in both data centers):

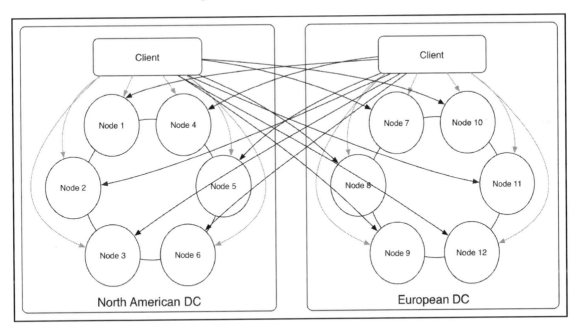

When non-local consistency levels are used, requests can be routed anywhere in the cluster.

Obviously sending traffic across the Atlantic Ocean will have a serious impact on client performance, which is why it's so critical that application architects and operations personnel work together to make sure consistency levels match the deployed data center configurations. You can imagine how the situation could become even less tenable with the addition of more data centers!

As an alternative to the previous scenario, it is nearly always preferable to use a local consistency level (LOCAL_ONE, LOCAL_QUORUM, or LOCAL_SERIAL) to ensure you're only working against the local data center, resulting in a far more performant configuration:

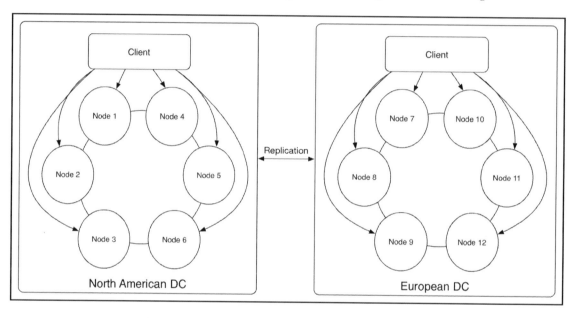

When using local consistency levels, requests are sent only to nodes in the specified data center.

When using this strategy, you must make sure your client is only aware of the local nodes. If you're using the native Java driver, you can read about how to do this in Chapter 6, *High Availability Features in the Native Java Client*. Otherwise, consult the documentation for the driver you are using, or consider moving to one of the newer native drivers.

Note that it is not sufficient to simply provide your client with the local node list and then attempt to use a global consistency level (ALL, ONE, TWO, THREE, QUORUM, or SERIAL). This is because once the operation hits the database, Cassandra will not restrict fulfillment of the consistency requirements to the local data center. If you intend to satisfy the consistency guarantee locally, you must use a local consistency level (LOCAL_ONE, LOCAL_QUORUM, or LOCAL_SERIAL).

Additionally, if your client connects to a remote node using a local consistency level, the consistency level will be fulfilled using nodes in the remote data center. This is because locality is measured relative to the coordinator node, not to the client.

Anatomy of a replicated write

It is important to fully grasp what's going on when you perform a write in a multiple data center environment in order to avoid common pitfalls and make sure you achieve your desired consistency goals.

To start, we will assume your clients generally need to be aware of updates as soon as they are written. We have discussed the fact that it's possible to achieve strong consistency using QUORUM reads and writes, but what happens in the case of LOCAL_QUORUM, which is typically the suggested default? Let's examine this situation in detail.

We will assume we have two live data centers in a geographically distributed configuration, one in North America and the second in Europe. Each data center has a client application that's responsible for performing reads and writes local to that data center, using LOCAL_QUORUM for both.

We have established that local reads and writes will be strongly consistent (refer to `Chapter` `3`, *Replication*, for a review of the reasons behind this), so the question is, what consistency guarantees do we have between data centers?

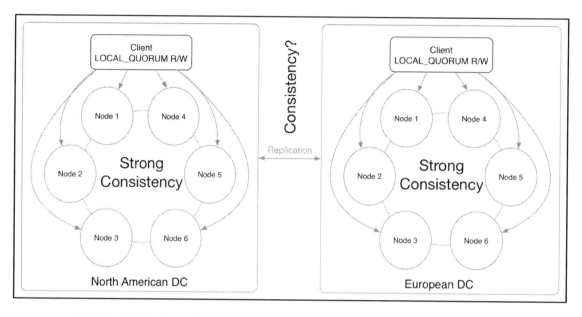

With LOCAL_QUORUM reads and writes, data inside a data center is strongly consistent, but what happens to inter-data center consistency?

To answer this question, let's examine the high-level path a write takes from the time the client sends it to Cassandra:

1. The client sends a write request using the `LOCAL_QUORUM` consistency level.
2. The node that receives the request (the coordinator) is responsible for insuring the consistency level guarantees are met prior to acknowledging the write.
3. The coordinator determines the nodes that should own the replicas using consistent hashing (see `Chapter 2`, *Data Distribution* for more details) and then sends the writes to those nodes, including one in each remote data center, which then acts as coordinator inside that data center.
4. Since we're using `LOCAL_QUORUM`, the coordinator will only wait for a majority of replica owning nodes in the local data center to acknowledge the write. This implies that there may be remote down hosts who have not yet received the write and are therefore inconsistent.

If you were paying close attention to the flow, you may have noticed that step 4 included a guarantee that at least a majority of local nodes received the write, so we know that a LOCAL_QUORUM read will result in strong consistency within the same data center. However, there was no guarantee that any remote writes succeeded. In fact, it's entirely possible that only the local data center was operational at the time of the request.

> Based on the Cassandra write path, we must conclude that LOCAL_QUORUM writes inside a data center exhibit strong consistency when paired with LOCAL_QUORUM reads, whereas the same pattern results in eventual consistency *between* data centers.

Thus, we can complete our diagram as follows:

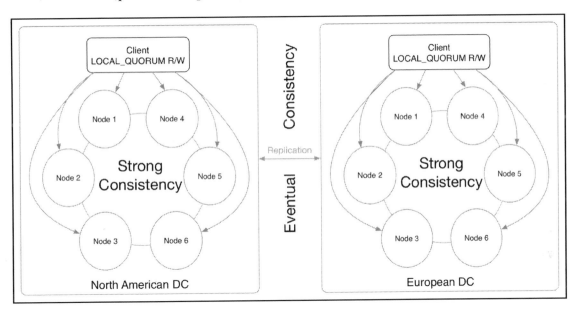

With LOCAL_QUORUM reads and writes, we get eventual consistency between data centers.

This level of guarantee is appropriate for many use cases, especially where users are being routed to a single data center the vast majority of the time. In this instance, eventual consistency would be acceptable, since traveling across continents takes enough time that the second data center would have received the writes by the time the individual had completed their travels.

But in some cases you may want or need to guarantee consistency in a remote data center, but you cannot afford to pay the cost by using a global consistency level at write time.

Achieving stronger consistency between data centers

There are a number of reasons why you may want to know for sure that your remote data is consistent with the originating data center. For example, you may need to ensure that your analytics include the most up-to-date data, or you might be reconciling bank transactions that occurred in another data center. Either way, you want to know prior to running your analysis or reconciliation job that your data is as recent as possible.

The solution to this dilemma is to run `nodetool repair` more frequently. Typically, it is advised that users run a repair at least once every `gc_grace_seconds`, but this is only an upper bound. If you want to make sure a remote data center is as consistent as possible, you can choose to run repairs more frequently, as this will make sure all your data is consistent with the originating data center.

 Always keep in mind when running repairs that the process is quite intensive, so be sure to stagger the process such that only a subset of your nodes is involved in a repair at any given time. If you must maintain availability during repairs, a higher replication factor may be needed to satisfy consistency guarantees.
You can choose to run incremental repairs, which can be run much more often as it is a much lighter weight process.

As we discussed in the first chapter, consistency in a distributed database is a complex and multi-faceted problem. This is even more the case when nodes in the database are dispersed across multiple geographical regions. Fortunately, as we have demonstrated, Cassandra provides the tools needed to handle this job.

The key to success in large-scale deployments of the sort we have covered in this chapter is to design your solution holistically. A common traditional approach to these problems has been to model the data independently of the infrastructure, then retrofit later to scale the solution.

You've likely chosen Cassandra because you have outgrown this approach, so don't make the mistake of applying old ideas to new technology. Consider how your replication factor, data center configuration, node counts, consistency levels, and analytics approach all work together to produce your desired result.

Summary

After reading this chapter and the previous one, you should have a solid understanding of how Cassandra ensures that your data is available when needed and protected from loss due to node or data center failure. By now you should be able to set up and configure a cluster across multiple geographical regions, and be familiar enough with data centers to begin the journey to analyzing your live data without cumbersome and expensive ETL processes.

So far we've focused on what it takes to get started with a solid Cassandra foundation for your application. In the next chapter, we will talk about what it looks like when your use case grows beyond your original plan and you need to scale out your cluster.

5
Scaling Out

In the old days, a significant increase in system traffic would cause excitement for the sales organization and strike fear in the hearts of the operations team. Fortunately, Cassandra makes the process of scaling out a relatively pain-free affair, so both your sales and operations teams can enjoy the fruits of your success.

This chapter will give you a complete rundown of the processes, tools, and design considerations when adding nodes or data centers to your topology. We will cover the following topics:

- Choosing the right hardware configuration
- Scaling out versus scaling up
- Adding nodes
- The bootstrapping process
- Adding a data center
- How to size your cluster correctly

It should go without saying that making proper choices regarding the underlying infrastructure is a key component to achieving good performance and high availability. Conversely, poor choices can lead to a host of issues, and recovery can sometimes be difficult.

Let's begin the chapter with some guidance on choosing hardware that's compatible with Cassandra's design.

Choosing the right hardware configuration

There are a number of points to consider when deciding on a node configuration, including disk sizes, memory requirements, and number of processor cores. The right choices here depend quite a bit on your use case and whether you are on physical or virtual infrastructure, but we will discuss some general guidelines here.

Since Cassandra is designed to be deployed in large-scale clusters on commodity hardware, an important consideration is whether to use fewer large nodes or a greater number of smaller nodes.

Regardless of whether you're using physical or virtual machines, there are a few key principles to keep in mind:

- **More RAM equals faster reads**, so the more you have the better they will perform. This is because Cassandra can take advantage of its cache capabilities as well as larger memory tables. More space for memory tables means fewer scans to the on-disk SSTables. More memory also results in better filesystem caching, which reduces disk operations.
- **... but not if you allocate it to JVM heap**. Most of the time, the default JVM heap size is sufficient, as Cassandra stores its $O(n)$ structures (those that grow with data set size) off-heap. In general, you should not use more than 8GB of heap on the JVM.
- **More processors equal faster writes**. This is because Cassandra is able to efficiently utilize all available processors, and writes are generally CPU-bound. While this may seem counter-intuitive, it holds true because Cassandra's highly efficient log-structured storage introduces so little overhead.
- **Disk utilization is highly dependent on data volume and compaction strategy**. Obviously, you will need more disk space if you intend to store more data. What may be less obvious is the dependence on your compaction strategy. In the worst case, `SizeTieredCompactionStrategy` can use up to 50% more disk space than the data itself. As an upper bound, try to limit the amount of data on each node to 1-2 TB.
- **Solid-state drives are a good choice**. For many use cases, simply moving to SSDs from spinning disks can be the most cost effective way to boost performance. In fact, SSDs should be the default choice since they provide tremendous benefits without any real drawbacks.

- **Do not use shared storage**, because Cassandra is designed to use local storage. Shared storage configurations introduce unwanted bottlenecks and subvert Cassandra's peer-to-peer design. They also introduce an unnecessary single point of failure.
- **Cassandra needs at least two disks**, one for the commit log and one for data directories. This is somewhat less important when using SSDs, as they handle parallel writes better than spinning disks.

For physical hardware, between 16 GB and 64 GB of RAM seems to be a good compromise between price and performance, whereas 16 GB should be considered ideal for virtual hardware. When choosing the right number of CPUs, 8-core processors are currently a good choice for dedicated machines. CPU performance varies among cloud vendors, so it's a good idea to consult the vendor and/or perform your own benchmarks.

These simple guidelines will help you to get the most out of your hardware or cloud infrastructure investment, and form a solid foundation for a high-performance and highly available cluster.

Scaling out versus scaling up

So you know it's time to add more muscle to your cluster, but how do you know whether to scale up or out?

If you're not familiar with the difference, scaling up refers to converting existing infrastructure to better or more robust hardware (or instance types in cloud environments). This could mean adding storage capacity, increasing memory, moving to newer machines with more cores, and so on.

Scaling out simply means adding more machines that roughly match the specifications of the existing machines. Since Cassandra scales linearly with its peer-to-peer architecture, scaling out is often more desirable.

In general, it is better to replace physical hardware components incrementally rather than all at one time. This is because in large systems failures tend to come after hardware ages to a certain point, which is statistically likely to happen simultaneously for some subset of your nodes. For example, purchasing a large lot of drives from a single source at one time is likely to result in a sudden onslaught of drive failures as they near the end of their service life.

How do you know which is the better strategy? To arrive at an answer, you should ask yourself a few questions about your existing infrastructure:

1. Have there been significant advances in hardware (or cloud instance types, in the case of EC2, Google Cloud, and so on), such that scaling up yields more benefit for the cost than adding nodes? Refer to this excellent article from Netflix, where they discuss the benefits of moving to **Solid State Disk (SSD)** rather than adding nodes: http://techblog.netflix.com/212/7/benchmarking-high-performance-io-with.html.

2. Did you start with hardware that was too small, because you were bound by the limitations of early Cassandra versions or a cloud provider's offerings at the time?

3. Do you have existing hardware to repurpose for use as a Cassandra cluster that is better than your current hardware?

If the answer to any of the above questions is yes, then scaling up may be your best option. If the answer is no, it may still be better to scale up, depending on what extra resources you hope to gain by scaling up and the cost-benefit ratio. If, for example, you only need more storage but not more CPU or IOPS, then adding disks is probably cheaper. If you need a bit more memory for cache, then add some memory if your nodes can take more.

But upgrading the motherboard to take more memory is unlikely to be cost effective, so adding nodes is a better choice. Fortunately, Cassandra makes scaling out painless. Regardless of which path you choose, you will need to know how to add nodes to your cluster.

Growing your cluster

The process of adding a node to an existing Cassandra cluster ranges from trivial when vnodes are used to somewhat tedious if you are manually assigning tokens. Let's start with the manual case, as the vnodes process is a subset of this.

Adding nodes without vnodes

As previously mentioned, the procedure for adding a node to a cluster without vnodes enabled is straightforward, if not a bit tedious. In general, you should add one node at a time, unless you're able to double the size of the cluster. Doubling removes the need to reassign tokens, as Cassandra's default of bisecting another node's range will be sufficient. The first step is to determine the new total cluster size, then compute tokens for all nodes.

To compute tokens, follow the DataStax documentation at `http://www.datastax.com/doc umentation/cassandra/1.2/cassandra/configuration/configGenTokens_c.html`. There are also several useful online tools to help you, such as this one at `http://www.gerob a.com/cassandra/cassandra-token-calculator/`.

Once you have the new tokens, complete the following steps to add your new nodes to the cluster:

1. If possible, run repairs to ensure all nodes contain the most recent data.
2. Make sure Cassandra is installed, but do not start the process. If you use a package manager, be aware that Cassandra will start automatically, so you will need to stop the process before proceeding.
3. On new nodes, in `cassandra.yaml`, set the addresses to their proper values, along with the cluster name, seeds, and endpoint snitch. Then set the `initial_token` value to the node's assigned token, using the tokens calculated prior to beginning this process.
4. Start the Cassandra daemon on the new node.
5. Wait for the node to complete its bootstrap before moving on to the next node. You can use `nodetool netstats` to check the status of the bootstrap process.
6. Once all new nodes are up, run `nodetool move` on old nodes to assign new tokens on one node at a time. This is unnecessary if you are doubling the cluster size, as the token assignments on old nodes will remain the same.
7. After this process has been completed on all new and existing nodes, run `nodetool cleanup` on old nodes to purge old data that now belongs to the new nodes. You should do this on one node at a time.

Adding nodes with vnodes

The primary difference when using vnodes is that you do not have to generate or set tokens, as this happens automatically, and there is no need to run `nodetool move`. Instead of setting the `initial_token` property, you should set the `num_tokens` property in accordance with the desired data distribution. Larger values represent proportionally larger nodes in your cluster, with 256 being the default. If all your nodes are the same size, this default should be sufficient.

Over time, your cluster may naturally become heterogeneous in terms of node size and capacity. In the past, when using manually assigned tokens, this presented a challenge, as it was difficult to determine the proper tokens that would result in a balanced cluster.

With vnodes, you can simply set the `num_tokens` property to a larger number for larger nodes. For example, if your typical node owns 256 tokens, when adding a node with twice the capacity, you should set its `num_tokens` property to 512.

If you want to keep track of the bootstrapping process, you can run `nodetool netstats` to view the progress. Once the streaming has completed, the output of this command will look similar to this:

```
Mode: NORMAL
Not sending any streams.
Read Repair Statistics:
Attempted: 1
Mismatch (Blocking): 0
Mismatch (Background): 0
Pool Name                   Active      Pending       Completed
Commands                      n/a            0               1
Responses                     n/a            0           12345
```

Once the `Mode` status reports as `NORMAL`, this indicates the node is ready to serve requests. If bootstrapping fails for any reason (often due to heavy load on one of the source nodes, which may result in timeouts), you can use `nodetool bootstrap resume` to continue the bootstrap process while skipping already streamed data. This can save a significant amount of time on large nodes.

Now that you know how to add a node, let's examine the two paths to increasing the capacity of your cluster, starting with scaling out.

Adding a data center

Scaling out typically involves adding nodes to your current cluster, but may also mean adding an entire data center. If you simply need to add nodes to an existing data center, you may have guessed that you must only follow the steps for adding a node, as described in the previous section on that topic.

Adding a new data center to your cluster is similar to initializing a new multi-node cluster. As this is not a basic tutorial on Cassandra, we will assume you already know how to do this. Before starting your nodes in the new data center, make sure to keep in mind the following additional details:

- **You must use NetworkTopologyStrategy with an appropriate snitch**: If you have not already chosen a data center-aware snitch, the recommendation is to use the `GossipingPropertyFileSnitch` for non-EC2 installations or the `EC2MultiRegionSnitch` for EC2 installations. See `Chapter 4`, *Data Centers* for more information on configuring snitches.
- **Set auto_bootstrap to false in cassandra.yaml**: This property is set to `true` by default, and if left as `true` will cause the node to immediately start transferring data from the existing data center. The correct procedure is to wait and run a rebuild after all nodes are online.
- **Configure the seeds**: It is a good idea to include at least a couple nodes from each data center as seeds in `cassandra.yaml`.
- **Update the appropriate properties files**: If you're using the `GossipingPropertyFileSnitch`, add the `cassandra-rackdc.properties` file on each new node. If you have chosen the `PropertyFileSnitch`, you will need to update `cassandra-topology.properties` on ALL nodes (a restart is not required on existing nodes).

Prior to changing your keyspace definition, be sure to change the consistency levels on your clients so they reflect the desired guarantees. Failing to do this may result in slow response times and `UnavailableException` as Cassandra attempts to satisfy the target consistency level using your new data center.

This is especially true when moving from a single data center environment (where your calls are likely, for example, to be QUORUM rather than LOCAL_QUORUM). When adding data centers beyond the second, it should be less of a concern. See `Chapter 6`, *High Availability Features in the Native Java Client* for more details if you're using the native driver.

Once your new nodes are online, you will need to change your keyspace properties to reflect your desired replication factor for each data center. For example, suppose you previously had a data center named DC1 and your new data center is called DC2. If you wanted both DC1 and DC2 to have three replicas, you would issue the following command:

```
ALTER KEYSPACE [your_keyspace]
WITH REPLICATION = {
  'class' : 'NetworkTopologyStrategy',
  'DC1' : 3,
  'DC2' : 3
}
```

Note that you only need to do this on one node, as your schema will be gossiped to all nodes in all data centers.

After you have set your desired replication factor, you will need to execute a rebuild operation on each node in the new data center:

```
nodetool rebuild -- [name of data center]
```

The `rebuild` will ensure that nodes in the new data center receive up-to-date replicas from the existing data center. It's important to include the data center name when issuing this command, or the rebuild operation will not copy any data. You can safely run this on all nodes at once, provided your existing data center can handle the additional load. If you are in doubt about this, it may be wise to run the rebuild on one node at a time to avoid potential problems.

How to scale up

Properly scaling up your Cassandra cluster is not a difficult process, but it does require you to carefully follow established procedures to avoid undesirable side effects. There are two general approaches to consider:

- **Upgrade in place**: To upgrade in place involves taking each node out of the ring, one at a time, bringing its new replacement online, and allowing the new node to bootstrap. This choice makes the most sense if a subset of your cluster needs upgrading rather than an entire data center. This assumes, of course, that your replication factor is greater than ONE. To upgrade an entire data center, it may be preferable to allow replication to automatically build the new nodes.

- **Using data center replication**: Since Cassandra already supports bringing up another data center via replication, you can use this mechanism to populate your new hardware with existing data and then switch to the new data center when replication is complete.

Upgrading in place

If you have determined that your best strategy is to upgrade a subset of your existing nodes, you will need to take the node offline so the cluster sees its status as down, which can be confirmed using `nodetool status`:

```
Datacenter: dc1
Status=Up/Down
|/ State=Normal/Leaving/Joining/Moving
--  Address        ...
UN  10.10.10.1  ...
UN  10.10.10.2...
DN  10.10.10.3      ...
UN  10.10.10.4      ...
```

You can see in this excerpt from the output that the node at address `10.10.10.3` is labeled `DN`, which indicates that Cassandra sees it as down. Once you have confirmed this, you should make a note of the address (and the token if you are using manually assigned tokens).

You are now ready to begin the process of replacing the node, which simply involves following the previously outlined steps for adding a node, with the following minor exceptions:

- With a packaged installation, add this line to `/usr/share/cassandra/cassandra-env.sh` prior to starting Cassandra:

  `JVM_OPTS="$JVM_OPTS -Dcassandra.replace_address=[old_address]`

- With a tarball installation, when starting Cassandra, use the following option:

  bin/cassandra -Dcassandra.replace_address=[old_address]

You will need to repeat this process for each node you want to upgrade, and make sure to execute the procedure one node at a time. In addition, you should consider running a repair after each node replacement. If only two of three nodes contain the latest data for some particular token range, and you're replacing one of these nodes, Cassandra might end up copying the data from the node with the older data. Then you would only have the latest data on one node. If that node is replaced next, you would lose that data.

Scaling up using data center replication

If you have a large data center and intend to replace all the hardware in that data center, the simplest way to handle this is to use Cassandra's replication mechanism to do the hard work for you. Once the new data center is ready to receive traffic, you can then simply redirect client requests to it. At that point you will be able to safely decommission the old data center.

To accomplish this, you should follow the procedure for adding a data center, which is outlined earlier in this chapter. Once your new data center is online, you should do the following:

1. Validate that all new nodes are online using `nodetool status`.
2. Redirect all client traffic to the new data center, and make sure there are no remaining clients connected to the old data center before proceeding.
3. Run `nodetool repair` on all keyspaces across the entire cluster to ensure any data that was updated on the old data center is propagated to the rest of the cluster.
4. Use the `ALTER KEYSPACE` command to remove any references to the old data center, as described in the earlier section on adding data centers.
5. Run `nodetool decommission` on each of the old nodes to permanently remove it from the cluster.

Removing nodes

While the material in this chapter is primarily focused on adding capacity to your cluster, there may be times when reducing capacity is what you're hoping to accomplish. There are a number of valid reasons for doing this. Perhaps you're experiencing smaller transaction volumes than originally anticipated for a new application, or maybe you've changed your data retention plan. In some cases you may want to move to a smaller cluster with more capable nodes, especially in cloud environments where this transition is made easier.

Regardless of your reasons for doing so, knowing how to remove nodes from your cluster will certainly come in handy at some point in your Cassandra experience. Let's take a look at this process now.

Removing nodes within a data center

Fortunately, the process for removing a node is quite simple:

1. Run `nodetool repair` on all your keyspaces. This will ensure that any updates which may be present only on the node you're removing will be preserved in the remaining nodes.
2. Presuming the node is online, run `nodetool decommission` on the node you're retiring. This process will move the retiring node's token ranges to other nodes in the ring and then copy replicas to their appropriate locations based on the new token assignments. As mentioned previously, you can use `nodetool netstats` to keep track of each node's progress during this operation.
3. If you're manually assigning tokens, you must reassign all your tokens so your distribution is even. This procedure is outlined in an earlier section in this chapter.
4. Validate that the node has been removed using `nodetool status`. If the node has been properly removed, it should no longer appear in the list output from this command.

Decommissioning a data center

If you want to remove an entire data center, the process closely mirrors what we outlined earlier in the section on scaling up via data center replication. For clarity, however, let's repeat just the important steps here:

1. Run `nodetool repair` on nodes in any other data centers (besides the one you're decommissioning) to ensure any data that was updated on the old data center is propagated to the rest of the cluster.
2. Use the `ALTER KEYSPACE` command to remove any references to the old data center, as described in the earlier section on adding data centers.
3. Run `nodetool decommission` on each of the old nodes to permanently remove it from the cluster.

Given the coordination required between multiple teams to successfully execute major topology changes, it is often advisable to appoint a single knowledgeable person who can oversee this process to ensure all the proper steps are taken. This simple step can help to avoid significant issues. Even better, automated cluster management tools such as **Puppet**, **Chef**, or **Priam** can make this process much easier.

By now you should be familiar with the various possible operations for adding and removing nodes or data centers. As you can see, these processes require planning and coordination between application designers, DevOps team members, and your infrastructure team. The consequences for improper execution of any of these processes can be quite substantial.

Other data migration scenarios

At times you may need to migrate large amounts of data from one cluster to another. A common reason for this is the need to transition data between networks that cannot see each other, or moving from classic Amazon EC2 to a newer **Virtual Private Cloud** (**VPC**) infrastructure.

If you find yourself in this situation, you can use these steps to ensure a smooth transition to the new infrastructure:

1. Set up your new cluster using the information you learned from this chapter, configure your cluster, and duplicate the schema from your existing cluster.
2. Change your application to write to both clusters. This is certainly the most significant change, as it likely requires code changes in your application.
3. Verify you are receiving writes to both clusters to avoid potential data loss.
4. Create a snapshot of your old cluster using the `nodetool snapshot` command.
5. Load the snapshot data into your new cluster using the `sstableloader` command. This command actually streams the data into the cluster rather than performing a blind copy, which means that your configured replication strategy will be honored.
6. Switch your application to point only to the new cluster.
7. Shut down the old cluster.

It's possible to skip the step that requires your application to direct traffic to both clusters, provided you can schedule sufficient downtime. The problem is that it's difficult to accurately predict how long the load will take, and considering the subject matter of this book it's likely that your application cannot sustain this downtime.

One final topic that's worth covering when talking about increasing cluster capacity is the possibility that you may need to change snitches. Often users will start with the SimpleSnitch, and then find they want to add a data center later, which requires one of the data center-aware snitches. If done incorrectly, snitch changes can be problematic, so let's discuss the proper way to handle this scenario.

Snitch changes

As you should recall from Chapter 4, *Data Centers*, the snitch tells Cassandra what your network topology looks like, and therefore, affects data placement in the cluster. If you haven't inserted any data, you can change the snitch without consequence. Otherwise multiple steps are required, as is a full cluster restart, which will result in downtime.

The following procedure should be used to change snitches:

1. Update your topology properties files, which means cassandra-topology.properties or cassandra-rackdc.properties, depending on which snitch you specify. In the case of the PropertyFileSnitch, make sure all nodes have the same file. For GossipingPropertyFileSnitch or EC2MultiRegionSnitch, each node should have a file indicating its place in the topology.
2. Update the snitch in cassandra.yaml. You will need to do this for every node in the cluster.
3. Restart all nodes, one at a time. Any time you make a change to cassandra.yaml, you must restart the node.
4. Change the replication strategy to NetworkTopologyStrategy for any keyspaces that are set to SimpleStrategy, and ensure that the data center you reference is consistent with the one you specified in step 1.

If you need to change your topology, you should change the snitch (by following the previously detailed steps) prior to making the changes. Once you have finished the snitch change procedure, you can then change your topology without needing to restart your nodes.

> If you're just starting out with Cassandra, it's best to plan for cluster growth from the beginning. Go ahead and choose either GossipingPropertyFileSnitch or the EC2MultiRegionSnitch (for EC2 deployments), as this will help avoid complications later when you inevitably decide to expand your cluster.

Summary

This chapter has covered quite a few procedures for handling a variety of cluster changes, from adding a single node, to expanding with a new data center, to migrating your entire cluster.

While it would be unreasonable to expect anyone to commit all these processes to memory, let this chapter serve as a reference for the times when these sometimes rare events occur. And perhaps most importantly, take note of these scenarios so you can know when it's time to read the manual rather than just trying to figure it out on your own. Distributed databases can be wonderful when handled correctly, but quite unforgiving when misused.

We've spent the last five chapters looking at a variety of mostly administrative and design related concepts, but now it's time to dig in and look at some application code. In the next chapter, we will take a look at the native client library (specifically the Java variant, although there are also drivers for C# and Python that follow similar principles).

The native driver has a number of interesting features related to high availability, so it's time to change into your developer hat as we transition from the database itself to the application layer. As you likely know from past experience, a properly architected client application is every bit as important as a correctly configured database.

6
High Availability Features in the Native Java Client

If you are relatively new to Cassandra, you may be unaware that the native client libraries from DataStax are a recent development. In fact, prior to their introduction there were numerous libraries (and forks of those projects) just for the Java language. Throw in the other languages, each with their own idiosyncrasies, and the situation was really quite dire.

Complicating the scenario was the lack of any universally accepted query mechanism, as **Cassandra Query Language (CQL)** was initially poorly received. The only real common ground for describing queries and data models was the underlying Thrift protocol. While this worked reasonably well for early adopters, it made assimilation of newer users quite difficult. It is a testament to Cassandra's extraordinary architecture, speed, and scalability that it was able to survive those early days.

After several revisions of CQL, the introduction of a native binary protocol, and DataStax's work on a modern CQL-based native driver, we are fortunately in a much better place now than we were just a couple of short years ago. In fact, the modern implementation of CQL is roughly 50 times faster than the equivalent Thrift query.

In this chapter, we will introduce the native Java driver and discuss its high availability features, covering the following topics:

- Thrift versus the native protocol
- Client basics
- Asynchronous requests
- Load balancing
- Failover policies
- Retries

While this chapter will focus specifically on Java implementation, there are also similar drivers for Python and C#. Though the specific implementation details may vary among languages, the basic concepts will prove useful no matter which driver you end up using.

It's also worth noting that in most cases it will be worth transitioning to the native Java driver if you're using another JVM-based language (such as Scala, Clojure, Groovy, and so on), even though your language of choice may have another community-supported Thrift-based driver available.

Thrift versus the native protocol

Cassandra users fall into two general categories:

- Those who have been using it a while and have grown accustomed to working directly with storage rows via a Thrift-based client.
- Those who are relatively new to Cassandra and are confused by the role Thrift plays in the modern Cassandra world.

Hopefully we can clear up the confusion and set both groups on the right path. Thrift is a **remote procedure call** (**RPC**) mechanism combined with a code generator, and for several years, it formed the underlying protocol layer for clients communicating with Cassandra. This allowed the early developers of Cassandra itself to focus on the database rather than the clients. But, as we hinted at in the introduction, there are numerous negative side effects of this strategy:

- There was no common language to describe data models and queries, as each client implemented different abstractions on top of the underlying Thrift protocol.
- Thrift was limited to the lowest common denominator, as implementation for all the supported languages, which proved to be a significant handicap as more advanced APIs became desirable.
- All requests were executed synchronously, as Thrift has no built-in support for asynchronous calls.
- All query results had to be materialized into memory on both the server and the client. This forced clients to implement cumbersome paging techniques when requesting large data sets to avoid exceeding available memory on either the client or the server. Limitations in the protocol itself also made optimization difficult.

For these reasons, the Thrift protocol is deprecated in favor of the newer binary protocol, which supports more advanced features such as cursors, batches, prepared statements, and cluster awareness, among others. In fact, the Thrift server is now disabled by default, and re-enabling it requires modifying `cassandra.yaml` or using `nodetool enablethrift`.

If you're still not convinced that you should migrate away from your favorite Thrift-based library, keep reading to learn about some of the great new features in the native driver. Even the popular Astyanax driver from Netflix now uses the native protocol under the hood.

Setting up the environment

To get the most out of this chapter, you should prepare your development environment with the following prerequisites:

- **Java Development Kit(JDK)** 1.8 for your platform, which can be obtained at `http://www.oracle.com/technetwork/java/javase/downloads/jdk8-downloads-2133151.html`.
- The **Integrated Development Environment(IDE)**, or text editor of your choice.
- Either a local Cassandra installation, or the ability to connect to a remote cluster.
- The DataStax native Java driver for your Cassandra version. If you're using Maven for dependency management, add the following lines to your `pom.xml` file:

```
<dependency>
  <groupId>com.datastax.cassandra</groupId>
  <artifactId>cassandra-driver-core</artifactId>
  <version>[version_number]</version>
</dependency>
```

Now that you're set up for coding, let's get familiar with some of the basics of the driver. The first step is to establish a connection to your Cassandra cluster, so we will start by doing just that.

Connecting to the cluster

To get connected, you will start by creating a `Cluster` reference, which you will then construct using a builder pattern. You will specify each additional option by chaining method calls together to produce the desired configuration, then finally calling the `build()` method to initialize `Cluster`.

Let's build a cluster that's initialized with a list of possible initial contact points:

```
private Cluster cluster; // defined at class level
// you should only build the cluster once per app
cluster = Cluster.builder()
    .addContactPoints("10.10.10.1", "10.10.10.2", "10.10.10.3")
    .build();
```

You should only have one instance of `Cluster` in your application for each physical cluster, as this class controls the list of contact points and key connection policies such as compression, failover, request routing, and retries.

While this basic example will suffice for playing around with the driver locally, the `Cluster` builder supports a number of additional options that are relevant for maintaining a highly available application, which we will explore throughout this chapter.

Executing statements

While the `Cluster` acts as a central place to manage connection-level configuration options, you will need to establish a `Session` to perform actual work against the cluster. This is done by calling the `connect()` method on your `Cluster` instance.

To run the following examples, you will need to create the `contacts` keyspace and `contact` table, as follows:

```
CREATE KEYSPACE contacts
WITH REPLICATION = {
    'class' : 'SimpleStrategy',
    'replication_factor' : 1
};

USE contacts;

CREATE TABLE contact (
    id UUID,
```

```
    email TEXT PRIMARY KEY
);
```

After the schema is created, you can connect to the `contacts` keyspace:

```
private Session session; // defined at class level
session = cluster.connect("contacts");
```

Once you have created the `Session`, you will be able to execute CQL statements, as follows:

```
String insert = "INSERT INTO contact (id, email) " +
                "VALUES (" +
                "bd297650-2885-11e4-8c21-0800200c9a66," +
                "'contact@example.com' " +
                ");";
session.execute(insert);
```

You can submit any valid CQL statement to the `execute()` method, including schema modifications.

> Unless you have a large number of keyspaces, you should create one
> `Session` instance for each keyspace in your application, because it
> provides connection pooling and controls the node selection policy (it uses
> a round robin approach by default). The `Session` is thread-safe, so it can
> be shared among multiple clients.

Prepared statements

One key improvement provided by the native driver is its support for prepared statements. Readers with a background in traditional relational databases will be familiar with the concept. Essentially, the statement is pre-parsed at the time it is prepared, with placeholders left for parameters to be bound at execution time.

Using the driver's `PreparedStatement` is straightforward:

```
String insert = "INSERT INTO contacts.contact (id, email) " +
                "VALUES (?,?);";
PreparedStatement stmt = session.prepare(insert);
BoundStatement boundInsert = stmt.bind(
    UUID.fromString("bd297650-2885-11e4-8c21-0800200c9a66"),
    "contact@example.com"
);
session.execute(boundInsert);
```

Use prepared statements whenever you need to execute the same statement repeatedly, as this will reduce parsing overhead on the server. However, do not create the same prepared statement multiple times, as this will actually degrade performance. You should prepare statements only once and reuse them for multiple executions.

Batched statements

It is also possible to use prepared statements with batches. When statements are grouped into a batch, they are executed atomically and without multiple network calls. This can be useful when you need either all or none of your statements to succeed.

Here's an example of preparing and executing a batch, using the statement prepared in the last code snippet:

```
BatchStatement batch = new BatchStatement();
batch.add(stmt.bind(
    UUID.fromString("bd297650-2885-11e4-8c21-0800200c9a66"),
    "contact@example.com"
));
batch.add(stmt.bind(
    UUID.fromString("a012a000-2899-11e4-8c21-0800200c9a66"),
    "othercontact@example.com"
));
session.execute(batch);
```

Caution with batches

While batches can be quite useful when they're needed, you should be aware of some pitfalls associated with them:

- **They are atomic, but not isolated**: This means clients will be able to see the incremental updates as they happen. The exception is updates to a single partition, which are isolated.
- **They are slower**: Specifically, the atomicity guarantee introduces approximately a 30% performance penalty across the batch. Sometimes this is worth it, but it means you shouldn't automatically assume batching multiple requests is better than multiple single requests. To avoid this penalty you can use unlogged batches, which turn off atomicity and provide increased performance over multiple statements executed against the same partition.

- **They are all or nothing**: In other words, either all statements fail or all succeed. This has the effect of increasing latency, as you have to wait for responses for all statements.
- **They are unordered**: Batching applies the same timestamp to all mutations in the batch, so statements don't actually execute in the provided ordering.

- **Be careful when using them with prepared statements to update many sparse columns**: It's tempting to prepare a single statement with a number of parameters for use in a large batch. This works fine if you always supply all the parameters, but don't assume you can insert nulls for missing columns, as inserting nulls creates tombstones. See `Chapter 8`, *Anti-Patterns* for details on why creating large numbers of tombstones is an anti-pattern.

Now that you're familiar with the basic client concepts, it's time to delve into the more advanced features, beginning with the ability to execute requests asynchronously.

Handling asynchronous requests

Since Cassandra is designed for significant scale, it follows that most applications using it would be designed with similar scalability in mind. One principal characteristic of high performance applications is that they do not block unnecessarily, and instead attempt to maximize available resources.

As previously discussed, one of the downsides to the older Thrift protocol was its lack of support for asynchronous requests. Fortunately, this situation has been remedied with the native driver, making the process of building scalable applications on top of Cassandra significantly easier.

 Blocking on I/O, such as with calls to Cassandra, can cause significant bottlenecks in high-throughput applications. Since a slow application can be the same as a dead application, you should use the asynchronous API to avoid blocking whenever possible.

If you are familiar with the `java.util.concurrent` package, and the `Future` class specifically, the asynchronous API will look familiar. Here's a basic example:

```
String query = "SELECT * FROM contact " +
    "WHERE id = bd297650-2885-11e4-8c21-0800200c9a66;";
ResultSetFuture f = session.executeAsync(query);
ResultSet rs = f.getUninterruptibly();
```

Obviously this is a naÃ¯ve example, as it will simply block on call to `getUninterruptibly()`, but it should give you a sense for the basic API.

Running queries in parallel

One common use case for the asynchronous API is to make multiple calls in parallel, then collect the results. This can be accomplished easily:

```
String query = "SELECT * FROM contact WHERE id = ?;";
BoundStatement q1 = session.prepare(query).bind(
    UUID.fromString("bd297650-2885-11e4-8c21-0800200c9a66")
);
BoundStatement q2 = session.prepare(query).bind(
    UUID.fromString("a012a000-2899-11e4-8c21-0800200c9a66")
);
ResultSetFuture f1 = session.executeAsync(q1);
ResultSetFuture f2 = session.executeAsync(q2);

try {
    ResultSet rs1 = f1.getUninterruptibly(5, TimeUnit.SECONDS);
    ResultSet rs2 = f2.getUninterruptibly(5, TimeUnit.SECONDS);
    // do something with results
} catch (Exception e) {
    // handle exception
}
```

A closer inspection of the `ResultSetFuture` class reveals that it inherits from both `java.util.concurrent.Future` and `com.google.common.util.concurrent.ListenableFuture` (which is from Google's Guava library). Guava's `Futures` class provides a useful construct for collecting multiple `Future` results into a single list of values, which can be helpful when aggregating queries. It can be used as follows:

```
Future<List<ResultSet>>future = Futures.allAsList(
    session.executeAsync(q1),
    session.executeAsync(q2)
);
try {
    List<ResultSet> results = future.get(5, TimeUnit.SECONDS);
    // do something with results
} catch (Exception e) {
    // handle exception
}
```

While the code above is more straightforward, there is one disadvantage to doing it this way. A call to `ResultSetFuture.getUninterruptibly()` will throw helpful Cassandra-specific exceptions, while `Future.get()` throws the more generic `ExecutionException` and `TimeoutException`. It's also worth noting that the `Future` returned by `allAsList()` will only be successful if all component `Future` succeed.

Load balancing

Since Cassandra is a distributed database with the ability to add and remove nodes easily, it's important for the client to be able to send requests to new nodes that join the cluster, or to stop sending requests to removed or dead nodes.

Some databases use special middle-man processes to broker requests to available nodes, thus relieving the client of the requirement to maintain a list of hosts. Since Cassandra is a peer-to-peer system, with no special nodes or broker processes, the client must be aware of the topology of the cluster.

> You should not use a load balancer between the client and Cassandra, as the client handles this via its load balancing policies. Adding a separate load balancer will actually prevent the client from understanding the cluster, which is what allows it to perform many of its duties.

Behind the scenes, the native driver connects to the cluster and learns about the topology of the ring. While legacy Thrift-based clients were able to make use of an RPC call to describe the cluster, the metadata obtained by the native client is much richer. You can get a good sense of the type of information available by taking a look at the `Metadata` class, which can be obtained by calling the `getMetadata()` method on your `Cluster` instance.

One of the chief strengths in this approach is that you can configure intelligent load-balancing and failover policies at the application level. Some policies act as wrappers around others, in a quasi-decorator pattern. Ultimately, the load balancer determines which node will end up coordinating the request. Internally, Cassandra will use its own mechanisms when communicating with the rest of the cluster.

The driver offers five load balancing policies out of the box:

- RoundRobinPolicy: As the name implies, this policy will execute requests in a round-robin fashion to all known nodes.
- DCAwareRoundRobinPolicy: This policy also executes in a round-robin fashion, but ensures that requests are routed only to hosts in the local data center. Keep in mind that this does **NOT** obviate the need to satisfy cross-data center consistency levels (such as QUORUM). It merely limits client connections to local nodes. This policy is the default lower-level policy and is typically wrapped by a higher-level implementation.
- LatencyAwarePolicy: If you want the driver to keep track of query latencies for each node, then route requests only to the fastest node, this policy will fit the bill. This policy acts as a wrapper around a child policy, and there are several properties you can set to tune its behavior.
- WhiteListPolicy: If you want the client to only talk to specific hosts, this policy will enable that behavior. However, it will not attempt to send requests to unavailable hosts.
- TokenAwarePolicy: This wrapper policy will make a best effort to select replicas for the given key in the local data center; otherwise, it will use the child policy to locate hosts.

The default combination of the DCAwareRoundRobinPolicy wrapped by the TokenAwarePolicy is a good place to start if you're unsure as to the right strategy. You should only add latency awareness as a tuning measure if you experience issues.

Let's examine some load balancing strategies in detail, and see how they might help us increase availability in the application.

Failing over to a remote data center

The foundation of any robust load balancing strategy is the DCAwareRoundRobinPolicy, because we'll assume you will be deploying to more than one data center. But the implementation hides an interesting failover feature that's worth a look.

In `Chapter 4`, *Data Centers*, we discussed several use cases for multiple data centers, with failover being one key scenario. If your desire is to failover to a backup data center should replicas in your client's primary data center fail, you may be interested in two additional options you can specify when building the `DCAwareRoundRobinPolicy`:

- `withUsedHostsPerRemoteDc`: This vaguely named method allows you to specify a number of hosts in a remote data center that can be used by this client should your local data center fail to satisfy the request. Note that by default, this will be ignored for `LOCAL_ONE` and `LOCAL_QUORUM` consistency levels.
- `allowRemoteDCsForLocalConsistencyLevel`: If set to `true`, this overrides the restriction on `LOCAL_ONE` and `LOCAL_QUORUM` requests. This should be enabled with caution, as it essentially breaks the consistency level policy. You should consider simply using another consistency level rather than enabling this feature.

Keep in mind that enabling fallback to remote hosts will likely result in degraded performance due to network latency, but this can be preferable to a wholesale failure of the application. A slow system and a down system often look the same, so you may be failing over to the remote data center even when all nodes in the local data center are up. The good news is that the policy is intelligent enough to make all possible efforts to satisfy requests locally before attempting to connect to remote nodes. In most cases, this only makes sense when using a numbered consistency level such as `ONE`, `TWO`, or `THREE`.

There is an important consideration when deciding whether to allow remote fallback. If you're relying on `LOCAL_QUORUM` reads and writes to maintain overall consistency, during the failover condition this consistency guarantee will be temporarily broken.

Downgrading consistency level

While failing over to a remote data center may be the right strategy in some cases, there is another option for dealing with potential node failures in the local data center. The driver offers a flexible retry policy interface that allows you to temporarily downgrade the consistency level during a failure.

For example, you may desire that your application write at a consistency level of `LOCAL_QUORUM` with a replication factor of three. If your client is unable to write to two replicas, the request will fail. In some cases, it may be preferable for the write to succeed on a single node, even if that results in potentially stale reads.

You can enable this feature with its default behavior by using the
DowngradingConsistencyRetryPolicy, like this:

```
private Cluster cluster; // defined at class level
cluster = cluster.builder()
    .addContactPoints("10.10.10.1", "10.10.10.2", "10.10.10.3")
    .withRetryPolicy(DowngradingConsistencyRetryPolicy.INSTANCE)
    .build();
```

Defining your own retry policy

It is also possible to specify your own behavior by implementing the RetryPolicy
interface. In the following naÃ¯ve example, we override the onReadTimeout() method to
always try at a consistency level of ONE as long as we have received at least one response
but not previously retried. For write timeouts, we defer to a default policy:

```
import com.datastax.driver.core.*;
import com.datastax.driver.core.exceptions.DriverException;
import com.datastax.driver.core.policies.*;

public class MyRetryPolicy implements RetryPolicy {
    private RetryPolicy defaultPolicy =
            DowngradingConsistencyRetryPolicy.INSTANCE;

    public MyRetryPolicy() {}

    public void init(Cluster cluster) {}
    public void close() {}

    @Override
    public RetryDecision onReadTimeout(Statement statement,
                                       ConsistencyLevel cl, int
                                       requiredResponses, int
                                       receivedResponses,
                                       boolean dataRetrieved, int nbRetry)
                                       {
        if (nbRetry != 0)
            return RetryDecision.rethrow();
        else if (receivedResponses > 0)
            return RetryDecision.retry(ConsistencyLevel.ONE);
        else
            return RetryDecision.rethrow();
    }

    @Override
    public RetryDecision onWriteTimeout(Statement stmt,
```

```
                                    ConsistencyLevel cl,
                                    WriteType type,
                                    int reqAcks, int recAcks,
                                    int nbRetry) {
        return defaultPolicy.onWriteTimeout(stmt, cl, type, reqAcks,
            recAcks, nbRetry);
    }

    @Override
    public RetryDecision onUnavailable(Statement stmt,
                                    ConsistencyLevel cl,
                                    int reqRep,int aliveRep,
                                    int nbRetry){
        return defaultPolicy.onUnavailable(stmt, cl, reqRep,
            aliveRep, nbRetry);
    }

    @Override
    public RetryDecision onRequestError(Statement stmt,
                                    ConsistencyLevel cl,
                                    DriverException exc,
                                    int nbRetry){
        return defaultPolicy.onRequestError(stmt, cl, exc, nbRetry);
    }

}
```

You can also override the methods for handling write timeouts (onWriteTimeout) and UnavailableException (onUnavailable). In many cases, however, the DowngradingConsistencyRetryPolicy will provide the desired functionality. Specifically, it will lower the consistency level on all operations such that they can be successful, but will attempt to maintain the highest level possible. Since exceptions are essentially overlooked in these cases, it can be helpful to wrap the handler in a LoggingRetryPolicy so you will know when exceptions occur.

A RetryPolicy can also be specified at the Statement level, which is often more useful than applying a one-size-fits-all policy globally:

```
Statement stmt = // create statement
session.execute(stmt.withRetryPolicy(
    DowngradingConsistencyRetryPolicy.INSTANCE));
```

If you decide to implement your own RetryPolicy, make sure to test it thoroughly under simulated failure conditions so you can be confident that it will behave as you believe it will.

Keep in mind that both failover policies and those that downgrade consistency level are a trade-off between consistency and availability. You will have to determine which is most important in any given circumstance. In many cases, it is a lesser of two evils decision, as neither situation may be ideal.

In general, you should be very careful when retrying to only do so at a single point in the call chain. For example, if client *A* calls service *B*, which then calls service *C*, which makes a request to Cassandra, ideally you should only perform retries in the outermost service. If all services implement retries, the number grows exponentially and can effectively result in a distributed denial-of-service attack from your own users.

Token awareness

With older Thrift-based drivers, the client is naive in regards to the location of the data in the cluster. It simply chooses a node (typically, randomly or using a round-robin scheme) and executes the query against that node. As a result, the coordinator often does not contain a replica for the requested key, which means additional nodes must participate to satisfy the request. The following diagram illustrates this point:

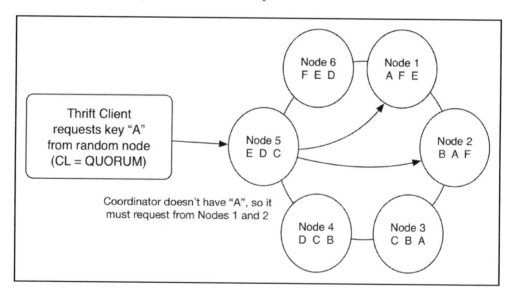

With a naive Thrift client, nodes are chosen at random, which often results in a situation where the coordinator doesn't have a copy of the data. So it must ask other nodes for replicas.

By contrast, much in the same way that the Hadoop and Spark drivers operate, the native driver is able to determine the token ranges owned by each node in the cluster. This is a significant advantage, as the TokenAwarePolicy load balancer can route requests to known owners of the requested key, rather than blindly choosing an available node. This can be visualized as follows:

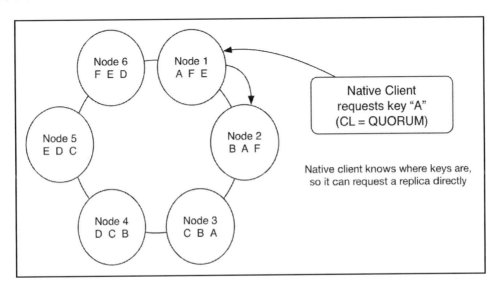

The native client can be configured to direct requests to one of the replica nodes, such that fewer total nodes are involved in fulfilling the request.

This feature is provided when using the TokenAware load balancing policy, which is enabled by default as of version 2.0.2 of the driver. You can enable it in previous versions like this:

```
private Cluster cluster; // defined at class level
LoadBalancingPolicy policy =
   new TokenAwarePolicy(DCAwareRoundRobinPolicy.builder().build());
cluster = cluster.builder()
    .addContactPoints("10.10.10.1", "10.10.10.2", "10.10.10.3")
    .withLoadBalancingPolicy(policy)
    .build();
```

In most cases, the TokenAwarePolicy is a great place to start. You will see the benefit in reduced latencies, as you avoid situations where the node that receives your request is unable to serve or write the replica, and therefore, must forward the request to one of the replica owners.

We have now covered all the pieces you need to maximize your application's ability to stay running during node failures. It's time to make use of these features in a cohesive strategy.

Tying it all together

In attempting to develop a comprehensive approach to handling failure, we will start by assuming you prefer consistency when possible, but want your application to remain available even if the desired consistency level cannot be satisfied. You are also willing to experience slower client response rather than denying requests.

With these ideas in mind, we can tie the concepts you have learned throughout this chapter together in a policy that answers this demand. Take a look at the following example, which makes use of the previously discussed features:

```java
// defined at class level
private String localDC = "DC1";
private ConsistencyLevel defaultCL =
  ConsistencyLevel.LOCAL_QUORUM;
private Cluster cluster;

LoadBalancingPolicy dcPolicy =
 DCAwareRoundRobinPolicy.builder()
  .withLocalDc(localDC)
  .withUsedHostsPerRemoteDc(2)
  .build();

// initialized once per application
cluster = cluster.builder()
   .addContactPoints("10.10.10.1", "10.10.10.2", "10.10.10.3")
   .withRetryPolicy(new LoggingRetryPolicy(
       DowngradingConsistencyRetryPolicy.INSTANCE))
   .withLoadBalancingPolicy(new TokenAwarePolicy(dcPolicy))
   .withQueryOptions(
     new QueryOptions().setConsistencyLevel(defaultCL))
   .build();
```

This implementation exhibits the following characteristics:

- If sufficient replicas exist in the local data center, both reads and writes will default to LOCAL_QUORUM, and therefore, queries will be strongly consistent.
- If sufficient replicas do not exist in the local data center, the consistency level will downgrade to either ONE, TWO, or THREE. The decision as to which is used is based on the highest level achievable that is at least one less than the originally requested level.
- Our DCAwareRoundRobinPolicy will continue to try to satisfy the consistency level using only local nodes if possible, avoiding unnecessary trips to the remote data center as long as the local data center can fulfill the downgraded consistency level.
- If all else fails, we have set the usedHostsPerRemoteDc parameter to two in the DCAwareRoundRobinPolicy. So if the local data center cannot produce a sufficient number of replicas to satisfy a consistency level of ONE, the policy allows it to contact a remote data center to fulfill the request.

Falling back to QUORUM

While this policy may fit the bill for many use cases, some users may prefer to initially fall back to QUORUM rather than ONE, TWO, or THREE. Consider that, at a replication factor of three, a LOCAL_QUORUM request will fall immediately to ONE using our previously proposed strategy, because only two replicas are necessary to satisfy the original consistency level.

The implication is that we have only one remaining live replica out of three in total, which could be considered a precarious situation. It is possible that both down replicas are in fact lost and that there may be some fundamental problem in the data center itself. In this case, if we fall back to writing at QUORUM instead of ONE, we are guaranteed to get at least one replica immediately persisted in a remote data center, thus protecting the write from a complete data center failure.

Unfortunately, there is no simpleconfiguration to enable this policy, so we must implement our own. As in the earlier example, we will simply use the DowngradingConsistencyRetryPolicy for most cases, since we really only want a slight modification of its behavior. Specifically, we need to override onUnavailable, as this controls the response when insufficient replicas are available to satisfy the requested consistency level. We let the default policy handle the timeout exceptions. Here's the implementation:

```java
import com.datastax.driver.core.*;
import com.datastax.driver.core.exceptions.DriverException;
import com.datastax.driver.core.policies.*;

public class QuorumFallbackPolicy implements RetryPolicy {
    private RetryPolicy defaultPolicy =
            DowngradingConsistencyRetryPolicy.INSTANCE;
    public static final RetryPolicy INSTANCE = new QuorumFallbackPolicy();

    private QuorumFallbackPolicy() {}

    public void init(Cluster cluster) { defaultPolicy.init(cluster); }
    public void close() { defaultPolicy.close(); }

    @Override
    public RetryDecision onUnavailable(Statement stmt,
                                       ConsistencyLevel cl,
                                       int reqRep,int aliveRep,
                                       int nbRetry){

        if (nbRetry == 0 && ConsistencyLevel.LOCAL_QUORUM == cl)
            return RetryDecision.retry(ConsistencyLevel.QUORUM);
        else if (nbRetry == 1)
            return RetryDecision.retry(ConsistencyLevel.ONE);
        else
            return defaultPolicy.onUnavailable(stmt, cl,reqRep,
                    aliveRep, nbRetry);
    }

    @Override
    public RetryDecision onReadTimeout(Statement stmt,
                                       ConsistencyLevel cl, int reqRes,
                                       int recRes,
                                       boolean dataRet, int nbRetry) {
        return defaultPolicy.onReadTimeout(stmt, cl, reqRes,
                recRes, dataRet, nbRetry);
    }

    @Override
```

```
public RetryDecision onWriteTimeout(Statement stmt,
                                    ConsistencyLevel cl,
                                    WriteType type,
                                    int reqAcks, int
                                    recAcks, int nbRetry) {
    return defaultPolicy.onWriteTimeout(stmt, cl, type, reqAcks,
            recAcks, nbRetry);
}

@Override
public RetryDecision onRequestError(Statement stmt,
                                    ConsistencyLevel cl,
                                    DriverException exc,
                                    int nbRetry){
    return defaultPolicy.onRequestError(stmt, cl, exc, nbRetry);
}
}
```

This retry policy first checks to see if the current consistency level is LOCAL_QUORUM and that this is the first retry. If so, it resets the level to QUORUM. If the QUORUM fails, onUnavailable() will be called again with the nbRetry count set to 1. In this case, the default is to simply throw the exception, so we need to check for nbRetry == 1 and do a second retry at consistency level ONE. Finally, it falls back to the default policy.

Note that this policy introduces a good bit of overhead in the failure case, as it allows for two retries (and therefore, three total calls per request). It would be advisable to monitor the number of failures, and simply start making calls at a different consistency level until the underlying cause of the failure condition is remedied. Otherwise, you will end up with numerous retries for each success, potentially compounding the issue.

In other words, use this strategy as an initial triage measure, but allowing it to continue for a long period of time could result in additional trouble.

Summary

In this chapter, you have learned the value of the native driver as a tool to assist you in developing a highly available application built on top of Cassandra. Hopefully it has been apparent that this objective involves a partnership between the application and the database, and that poor decisions on either end can dramatically affect availability.

However, the native driver has a wealth of functionality beyond what has been covered here, so it would be worth your while to spend some time understanding its features and subtleties, as with any new piece of software.

In Chapter 7, *Modeling for Availability* we will look at another aspect of designing highly available applications in Cassandra. We'll explore how the right data models can make or break your system, and what to do to ensure success.

7
Modeling for Availability

A well-designed data model is central to availability in Cassandra, while a poorly chosen model can substantially handicap your application's resiliency. This idea may seem counterintuitive to those with backgrounds in relational database systems, but this chapter may very well be the most critical one in this book.

It's not that data models are unimportant in relational systems, but they are especially critical when attempting to maintain availability in a large distributed database. In fact, this topic is probably the least understood and most difficult aspect of transitioning to Cassandra.

The data modeling problem is somewhat exacerbated by a familiar SQL-style syntax that can lure unsuspecting users into believing that they already understand the necessary principles. In reality, the similarity between **Contextual Query Language** (**CQL**) and SQL ends with syntax. The underlying data structure is vastly different, and therefore a new approach to designing your data model is required.

In this chapter, we will cover the fundamentals of successful data modeling in Cassandra, including the following topics:

- Understanding the storage layer
- Compaction
- Translating CQL to the storage layer
- Designing for immutability
- Modeling time series data
- Modeling geospatial data

After reading this chapter, you will understand the principles of effective data modeling, and hopefully the shroud of mystery surrounding CQL will be lifted. We'll begin by taking a look at Cassandra's on-disk data structure, as a solid grasp of this will allow you to understand why certain models work well while others do not.

How Cassandra stores data

Database systems use a variety of structures to represent data on disk. Most traditional relational systems use a tabular approach, which enables the kinds of random access queries supported by these systems. But in order to achieve Cassandra's hallmark write performance, it must avoid these sorts of random access disk seeks, because random disk I/O tends to be a significant bottleneck. Instead, the system employs a **log-structured storage engine**, which allows it to write data sequentially to both a **commit log** and Cassandra's permanent structure, **SSTables**.

Implications of log-structured storage

When a write is received, it is written simultaneously to the commit log and to an in-memory representation of the table, called a **memtable**. Note that the commit log is what provides durability of writes in Cassandra. Memtables are then periodically flushed to disk in the form of immutable SSTables.

Data in SSTables is split into partitions (which map to the primary key) and sorted in column name order. This is an important fact, which will be covered in greater detail later in this chapter. The commit log is only read on node restart to recover data not yet flushed to an SSTable.

This storage scheme has several important implications related to data modeling:

- **Writes are immutable**: Since writes are always essentially append operations, updating data involves simply writing the new value with a higher timestamp (every column is written with a timestamp attached to it).
- **The last write wins**: If multiple versions of a column exist on disk (as will be the case in an update), the latest value will be returned when that column is queried. All inserts are actually upserts, as there is no distinction between the two under the hood.

- **Columns cannot be physically deleted**: Immutability implies that data isn't actually deleted when a `DELETE` statement is executed. Instead, a `null` column value is inserted, covering up the old value. This value is referred to as a . Deletes and tombstones will be covered in detail in `Chapter 8`, *Anti-Patterns*.

- **Sequential queries are efficient**: Also referred to as range queries, any query that results in reading data sequentially on disk will maximize read performance, as it takes advantage of the underlying storage structure. In general, Cassandra restricts you to sequential queries, although there are several examples of queries that break this rule. We will look at range queries in this chapter, while other types will be dealt with in `Chapter 8`, *Anti-Patterns*.

One consequence of an append-only data structure is that old values must periodically be purged to avoid accumulating unnecessary junk data over time. For example, old values that have been replaced by newer ones should be purged. And since SSTables are immutable, we often end up with columns from the same partition existing in multiple files. This slows read performance, so we need a mechanism to manage this situation.

Understanding compaction

Cassandra deals with this build-up of SSTables over time by means of a process called **compaction**. Compaction aggregates partitions from multiple files into a single file, and in the process it removes old data and purges tombstones. But housekeeping is only one reason to do this; the other objective is to improve read performance by moving data for a given key into a single SSTable, thereby reducing the disk I/O required to read each key.

The exact mechanism that governs the compaction process depends on which compaction strategy you choose. As of version 3.8 (or 3.0.8, which added time-window compaction and deprecated date-tiered compaction), there are four strategies that ship with Cassandra (although you can implement your own):

- **Size-tiered compaction**: This strategy causes SSTables to be compacted when there are multiple files of a similar size (the default is four). In update-heavy workloads, a partition may exist in many SSTables at once, resulting in reduced read performance.

- **Leveled compaction**: This strategy assigns SSTables to levels, where each level represents tables that are 10 times larger than the next lower level. This guarantees that tables in the same level won't overlap, and results in the vast majority of rows being read from a single SSTable. This is good for read-heavy workloads, but if you don't perform updates or deletes, or query large ranges across a partition, the additional I/O may not be worth the cost.

- **Time-window compaction**: Added in 3.8, this strategy replaces the deprecated date-tiered compaction, which suffered from usability and performance issues. It groups SSTables by time bucket and expiration, thereby allowing the compaction process to simply drop expired tables and ignore old unexpired tables. This strategy can dramatically reduce cluster overhead for time series workloads.

- **Date-tiered compaction**: Deprecated as of 3.8 in favor of the more straightforward time-window strategy.

Let's look at these compaction strategies in detail so you can make an informed decision about which is right for your use case.

Size-tiered compaction

Size-tiered compaction has been around in Cassandra from the early days, and prior to version 1.0 it was the only available option. The basic premise is that SSTables are chosen for compaction based on size buckets.

When the compaction process finds multiple SSTables (the default is four) of a similar size, it will compact those tables into a single SSTable. Eventually, there will be four larger tables, which will be compacted again into one table.

The following diagram shows the progression through multiple passes of the compaction process:

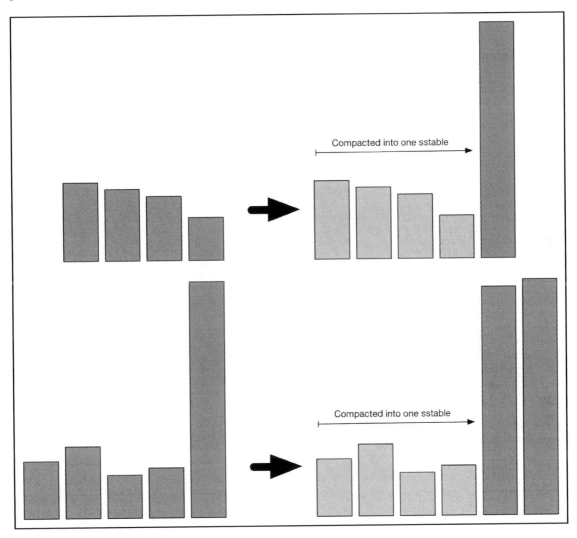

With size-tiered compaction, similarly sized tables are compacted into larger tables once a certain number are accumulated

Each stage results in smaller tables being combined into larger ones, such that ultimately after multiple compactions, the resulting SSTable distribution will resemble the following chart:

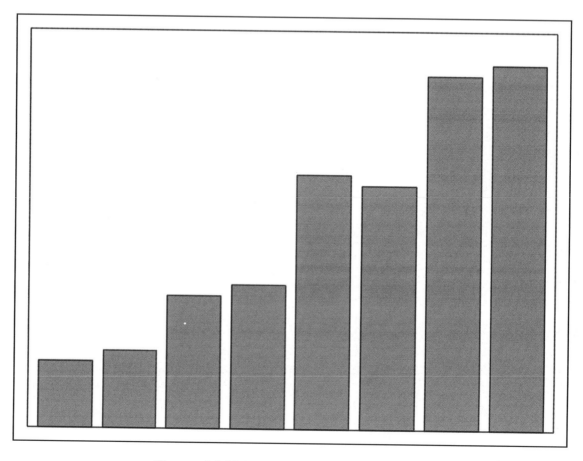

This represents the final distribution using size-tiered compaction after multiple passes

Size-tiered compaction has some disadvantages, which may or may not be important for your use case:

- **It can require a lot of extra disk space**, as much as twice the used disk space if there are no deletes or updates. This is because the tables are copied during compaction, so the data will be duplicated while the process is running. This is especially important for operations because it means you must have as much free space as your largest SSTables or they won't be able to compact.
- **A row can exist in multiple SSTables**, which can result in degradation of read performance. This is especially true if you perform many updates or deletes.

If you have very write-heavy workloads or your writes are generally immutable, size-tiered compaction can be a good strategy. Otherwise, you should probably choose leveled or time-window compaction.

Leveled compaction

Introduced in version 1.0, leveled compaction attempts to create SSTables that are fixed in size and then grouped into levels based on their size, with each level being 10 times the size of the previous level. A key trait of leveled compaction is that within a level, there are no overlapping SSTables. This minimizes the number of files that need to be checked in a given level, because a partition can only exist in at most one (and most likely zero) SSTable per level.

The algorithm is straightforward. New SSTables are placed in the first level, called **L0**, after which they are immediately compacted with the overlapping tables in the next level, **L1**. As L1 becomes filled, extra tables are merged with tables in **L2**, and so on.

This process introduces several improvements over size-tiered compaction for workloads involving lots of reads or updates:

- It uses much less space than size-tiered compaction, reducing the amount of disk space used while the SSTable is being compacted. Since SSTables are also much smaller using this strategy, this amounts to a reduction in space complexity.
- Much less space is wasted by old rows, at most 10%.
- Read performance is often improved, as 90% of all reads will require a lookup in only a single SSTable.

The leveled compaction strategy actually employs a hybrid approach, where the process switches to size-tiered compaction when Cassandra is unable to keep up with the load. The `max_threshold` property determines when this occurs.

Time-window compaction

Starting in versions 3.8 and 3.0.8, you can make use of a new time-window compaction strategy, which groups data into SSTables based on the write time and expiration. This can be helpful for time series models where the most frequent query patterns involve reading the most recent data. If you use TTLs, this strategy can group data expiring at the same time into the same SSTables, which allows it to simply remove the table without having to run compaction. Time-window compaction makes use of size-tiered compaction within windows, so it supports all the existing size-tiered configuration options.

Many users have reported significant gains in performance on time series workloads by switching to time-window compaction, and it is much easier to understand than its deprecated predecessor, date-tiered compaction. If you are running a version that has not yet incorporated time-window compaction, the upgrade is well worth the effort. Though it is a new strategy, many early adopters have been running it in production at scale for over a year, so you can proceed with confidence.

Compaction plays such a critical role in reducing disk usage and providing optimal read performance, making it important to choose the right strategy for your workload. As the compaction process can be intensive, you can choose to throttle it using the `compaction_throughput_mb_per_sec` setting in `cassandra.yaml`. The default is 16 MB/sec, which may be sufficient for many workloads. As with any tuning, you should measure the impact of compaction prior to changing this setting.

Now that you understand the high-level structure of Cassandra's storage engine, the next step is to examine how various data models translate to the underlying storage layer. These concepts will help you design models that take full advantage of Cassandra's unique characteristics.

CQL under the hood

At this point, most users should be aware that CQL has replaced Thrift as the standard (and therefore recommended) interface for working with Cassandra. Yet it remains largely misunderstood, as its resemblance to common SQL has left both Thrift veterans and Cassandra newcomers confused about how it translates to the underlying storage layer. This fog must be lifted if you hope to create data models that scale, perform, and ensure availability.

As we begin this section, it is important to understand that the CQL data representation does not always match the underlying storage structure. This can be challenging for those accustomed to Thrift-based operations, as those were performed directly against the storage layer. But CQL introduces an abstraction on top of the storage rows, and only maps directly in the simplest of schemas.

> If you want to be successful at modeling and querying data in Cassandra, keep in mind that while CQL improves the learning curve, it is not SQL. You must understand what's happening under the covers, or you will end up with data models that are poorly suited to Cassandra. As we'll discuss in Chapter 8, *Anti-Patterns*, indices are not always the answer.

So let's pull back the curtain and look at what our CQL statements translate to at the storage layer starting with a simple table.

Single primary key

The first model we will examine is a straightforward table, which we'll call `books`, with a single primary key called `title`:

```
CREATE TABLE books (
    title text,
    author text,
    year int,
    PRIMARY KEY (title)
);
```

We can then insert some data, as follows:

```
INSERT INTO books (title, author, year)
VALUES ('Patriot Games', 'Tom Clancy', 1987);
INSERT INTO books (title, author, year)
VALUES ('Without Remorse', 'Tom Clancy', 1993);
```

And finally we can read our newly inserted rows:

```
SELECT * FROM books;

  title            | author      | year
-----------------+------------+------
 Without Remorse | Tom Clancy | 1993
    Patriot Games | Tom Clancy | 1987
```

What we've done so far looks a lot like ANSI SQL, and in fact these statements would have been valid when run against most modern relational systems. But we know that something very different is happening under the hood.

At the storage layer, this data is represented by a row key, `title`, and a set of columns with `name` and `value`. Each column also has a `timestamp` that is used for conflict resolution. The following is a representation of the storage rows that closely resembles the old pre-3.0 CLI output, and we will continue with this representation throughout this chapter:

```
Row Key: Without Remorse
=> (name=author, value=Tom Clancy, timestamp=1393102991499000)
=> (name=year, value=1993, timestamp=1393102991499000)
Row Key: Patriot Games
=> (name=author, value=Tom Clancy, timestamp=1393102991499100)
=> (name=year, value=1987, timestamp=1393102991499100)
```

As you can see, this is nearly a direct mapping to the CQL rows. Let's point out a couple of important features of this data. First, you will recall from Chapter 2, *Data Distribution*, that the row key is distributed randomly using a hash algorithm, so the results are returned in no particular order. By contrast, columns are stored in sorted order by name, using the natural ordering of the type. In this case, `author` comes before `year` lexicographically, so it appears first in the list. These are critical points, as they are central to effective data modeling.

Compound keys

Now let's look at a slightly more complex example, one that uses a compound key. In this case, we'll create a new table, `authors`, with a compound key using `name`, `year`, and `title`:

```
CREATE TABLE authors (
    name text,
    year int,
    title text,
    isbn text,
    publisher text,
    PRIMARY KEY (name, year, title)
);
```

And this is what our data looks like after inserting two CQL rows:

```
name          | year | title           | isbn           | publisher
--------------+------+-----------------+----------------+----------
Tom Clancy | 1987 |    Patriot Games | 0-399-13241-4 |    Putnam
Tom Clancy | 1993 | Without Remorse | 0-399-13825-0 |    Putnam
```

This is where CQL can begin to cause confusion for those who are unfamiliar with what's happening at the storage layer. To make sense of this, it's important to understand the difference between **partition keys** and **clustering columns**.

Partition keys

When declaring a primary key, the first field in the list is always the partition key. This translates directly to the storage row key, which is randomly distributed in the cluster via the hash algorithm. Most queries require that you provide the partition key, so that Cassandra will know which nodes contain the requested data.

Clustering columns

The remaining fields in the primary key declaration are called clustering columns, and these determine the ordering of the data on disk. They are not, however, a part of the partition key, so they do not help determine the nodes on which the data will reside. But they play a key role in determining the kinds of queries you can run against your data, as we will see in the remainder of this section.

Thus, the breakdown of the fields in the primary key is as follows:

```
PRIMARY KEY (partition_key, clustering1, clustering2)
```

Now that you know the difference, it's time to see what our `authors` table looks like in its storage layer representation:

```
Row Key: Tom Clancy
=> (name=1987:Patriot Games:ISBN, value=0-399-13241-4)
=> (name=1987:Patriot Games:publisher, value=Putnam)
=> (name=1993:Without Remorse:ISBN, value=0-399-13825-0)
=> (name=1993:Without Remorse:publisher, value=Putnam)
```

You will note that our two CQL rows translated to a single storage row, because both of our inserts used the same partition key. But perhaps more interesting is the location of our `year` and `title` column values. They are stored as parts of the column name, rather than column values! Note that this is a simplified representation, as the new storage engine (as of 3.0) provides optimizations to avoid duplication of the clustering column names.

You can also observe that the rows are sorted first by `year` and then by `title`, which is the way we specified them in our primary key declaration. It is also possible to reverse the stored sort order by adding the WITH CLUSTERING ORDER BY clause, as follows:

```
CREATE TABLE authors (
    name text,
    year int,
    title text,
    isbn text,
    publisher text,
    PRIMARY KEY (name, year, title)
) WITH CLUSTERING ORDER BY (year DESC);
```

Then, when selecting our rows, we can see that the ordering starts with the latest year and ends with the earliest:

name	year	title	isbn	publisher
Tom Clancy	1993	Without Remorse	0-399-13825-0	Putnam
Tom Clancy	1987	Patriot Games	0-399-13241-4	Putnam

While this may seem to be a trivial point, it can matter a great deal depending on the types of queries you intend to run on your data. We will examine these implications later in this chapter when we discuss queries.

Composite partition keys

In the previous examples, we demonstrated the use of a single partition key with multiple clustering columns. But it's also possible to create a multi-part (or composite) partition key. The most common reason for doing this is to improve data distribution characteristics. A prime example of this is the use of time buckets as keys when modeling time series data. We will cover this in detail in the time series section of this chapter.

For now, let's see what it looks like to create a composite partition key:

```
CREATE TABLE authors (
    name text,
    year int,
    title text,
    isbn text,
    publisher text,
    PRIMARY KEY ((name, year), title)
);
```

The difference, in case it's not obvious, is the addition of parentheses around the `name` and `year` columns, which specifies that these two columns should form the composite partition key. This leaves `title` as the only remaining clustering column.

At the storage layer, this has the effect of moving the year from a component of the column name to a component of the row key, as follows:

```
Row Key: Tom Clancy:1993
=> (name=Without Remorse:isbn, value=0-399-13241-4)
=> (name=Without Remorse:publisher, value=5075746e616d)
--------------------
Row Key: Tom Clancy:1987
=> (name=Patriot Games:isbn, value=0-399-13825-0)
=> (name=Patriot Games:publisher, value=5075746e616d)
```

The 3.0 release introduced a significant refactor of the storage engine. Previously, the storage engine had no concept of CQL rows but rather represented data as a simple map of binary keys to binary cell blobs. The new engine understands the CQL rows, clustering columns, and type information, which allows for a number of improvements in both space and computational efficiency.

The importance of the storage model

You may be wondering why it matters how the data is stored internally. In fact, it matters a great deal for several important reasons:

- Your queries must respect the underlying storage. Cassandra doesn't allow ad hoc queries of the sort that you can perform using SQL on a relational system. If you don't understand how the data is stored, at best you will be constantly frustrated by the error messages you receive when you try to query your data, and at worst you will suffer poor performance.

- You must choose your partition key carefully, because it must be known at query time and must also distribute well across the cluster. Make sure to avoid models where even a small number of keys will contain huge numbers of columns, as this will impact data distribution.

- Because of its log-structured storage, Cassandra handles range queries very well. A range query simply means that you select a range of columns for a given key, in the order they are stored. Note that it is not possible to perform range queries across multiple partitions as they are located in physically different places on disk.

- You have to carefully order your clustering columns, because the order affects the sort order of your data on disk and therefore determines the kinds of queries you can perform.

Proper data modeling in Cassandra requires you to structure your data in terms of your queries. This is backward compared to the approach taken in most relational models, where normalization is typically the objective. With Cassandra, you must consider your queries first.

With these principles in mind, let's examine what happens when you run different kinds of queries so that you can better understand how to structure your data.

Understanding queries

In order to make sense of the various types of queries, we will start with a common data model to be used across the following examples. For this data model, we will return to the authors table, with name as the partition key, followed by year and title as clustering columns. We'll also sort the year in descending order. This table can be created as follows:

```
CREATE TABLE authors (
    name text,
    year int,
```

```
        title text,
        isbn text,
        publisher text,
        PRIMARY KEY (name, year, title)
) WITH CLUSTERING ORDER BY (year DESC);
```

Also, for the purposes of these examples, we will assume a replication factor of 3 and consistency level of QUORUM.

Query by key

We'll start with a basic query by key:

```
SELECT * FROM authors WHERE name = 'Tom Clancy';
```

For this simple select, the query makes the request to the coordinator node, which in this case owns a replica for our key. The coordinator then retrieves the row from another replica node to satisfy the quorum. Thus, we need a total of two nodes to satisfy the query:

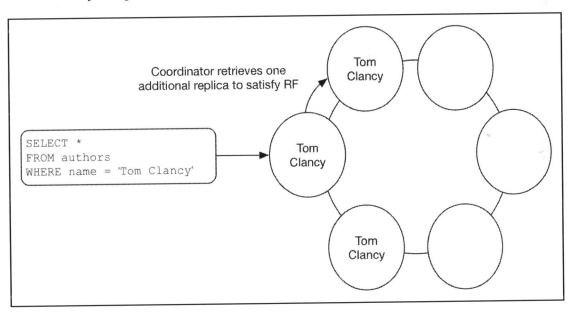

A simple query by key requires two nodes to satisfy a QUORUM read

At the storage layer, this query first locates the partition key and then scans all the columns in the natural sort order of the columns, as follows:

```
Row Key: Tom Clancy
=> (name=1996:Executive Orders:publisher, value=Putnam)
=> (name=1996:Executive Orders:ISBN, value=0-399-13825-0)
=> (name=1994:Debt of Honor:publisher, value=Putnam)
=> (name=1994:Debt of Honor:ISBN, value=0-399-13826-1)
=> (name=1993:Without Remorse:publisher, value=Putnam)
=> (name=1993:Without Remorse:ISBN, value=0-399-13825-0)
=> (name=1991:The Sum of All Fears:publisher, value=Putnam)
=> (name=1991:The Sum of All Fears:ISBN, value=0-399-13241-6)
...
=> (name=1987:Patriot Games:publisher, value=Putnam)
=> (name=1987:Patriot Games:ISBN, value=0-399-13241-4)
```

So, even though this appears to be a simple query by key, at the storage layer, it actually translates to a range query!

Range queries

If this basic query results in a range query, let's see what happens when we specifically request a range, like this:

```
SELECT * FROM authors WHERE name = 'Tom Clancy' AND year >= 1993;
```

In this case, we're still selecting a single partition, so the query must only check with two nodes as in the previous example. The difference is that in this case, Cassandra simply scans the columns until it finds one that fails the query predicate:

```
RowKey: Tom Clancy
    => (name=1996:Executive Orders:publisher, value=Putnam)
    => (name=1996:Executive Orders:ISBN, value=0-399-13825-0)
    => (name=1994:Debt of Honor:publisher, value=Putnam)
    => (name=1994:Debt of Honor:ISBN, value=0-399-13826-1)
    => (name=1993:Without Remorse:publisher, value=Putnam)
    => (name=1993:Without Remorse:ISBN, value=0-399-13825-0)
    => (name=1991:The Sum of All Fears:publisher, value=Putnam)
    => (name=1991:The Sum of All Fears:ISBN, value=0-399-13241-6)
    ...
    => (name=1987:Patriot Games:publisher, value=Putnam)
    => (name=1987:Patriot Games:ISBN, value=0-399-13241-4)
```

Once it finds the year 1991, Cassandra knows there are no more columns to scan. Therefore, this query is efficient because it must only read the required number of columns plus one.

To recap, there are three key points you should note from this discussion:

1. Sequential queries are efficient, because they take advantage of Cassandra's natural sort order at the storage layer.
2. Queries by key and combination of key plus clustering column are sequential at the storage layer, which of course means they are optimal.
3. Write your data the way you intend to read it. Put another way, model your data in terms of your queries and not the other way around. Following this rule will help you avoid the most common data modeling pitfalls that plague those who are transitioning from a relational database.

Now that we've covered the basics of how to build data models that make optimal use of the storage layer, let's look at how we can effectively leverage some of Cassandra's newer features to model for our queries.

Embracing denormalization

If you recall, earlier in this chapter we stated that you must write your data the way you intend to read it. Denormalization is the key, and Cassandra provides tools to help ease this burden.

If you come from a relational background, denormalization can initially be difficult to grasp. But it is extremely important, as normalized models tend to force applications to produce client-side joins. Using the authors table as an example, let's consider how we would model this in a normalized database.

We would of course start with an `authors` table, but the one-to-many relationship between `authors` and `books` would be modeled with a second table. Each table would have an ID, and the books table would have an `authorID` as a foreign key. The result would be similar to the following MySQL tables:

```
CREATE TABLE authors (
    authorID int,
    name varchar(50),
    PRIMARY KEY (authorID)
)

CREATE TABLE books (
    bookID int,
    authorID int,
    name varchar(100),
    year int,
    INDEX auth_ind (authorID),
    FOREIGN KEY (authorID) REFERENCES authors(authorID)
)
```

In a relational database we could execute a query joining these two tables together, which is a common operation. But imagine what would happen if we emulated this model in Cassandra. In order to retrieve a list of books and the associated author, we would have to request each book, then request the author separately, resulting in a query for each book plus the one for the author. This query would likely require many nodes to satisfy and would be very expensive to execute.

We need a saner model, and collections can help us solve this. An `authors` table with a collection of `books`, as in our earlier examples, gives us the ability to perform a single query to retrieve everything we need.

While it might be tempting to use secondary indices as a means of avoiding denormalizing your data, this is rarely a sound strategy. For more information on why this is the case, see `Chapter 8`, *Anti-Patterns*, where we cover secondary indices in detail.

Denormalizing using collections

The introduction of collections to CQL addresses some of the concerns that frequently arose regarding Cassandra's primitive data model. They add richer capabilities that give developers more flexibility when modeling certain types of data.

Cassandra supports three collection types: **sets**, **lists**, and **maps**. In this section, we will examine each of these and take a look at how they're stored under the hood. But first, it's important to understand some basic rules regarding collections:

- The size of each item in a collection must not be more than 64 KB
- A maximum of 64,000 items may be stored in a single collection
- Querying a collection always returns the entire collection
- Collections are best used for relatively small, bounded datasets

With these rules in mind, we can examine each type of collection in detail, starting with sets.

Sets

A set in CQL is very similar to a set in your favorite programming language. It is a unique collection of items, meaning it does not allow for duplicates. In most languages, sets have no specific ordering; Cassandra, however, stores them in their natural sort order, as you might expect.

Here is an example of a table of `authors` that contains a set of `books`:

```
CREATE TABLE authors (
    name text,
    books set<text>,
    PRIMARY KEY (name)
);
```

We can then insert some values as follows:

```
INSERT INTO authors (name, books)
VALUES ('Tom Clancy', {'Without Remorse', 'Patriot Games'});

UPDATE authors
SET books = books + {'Red Storm Rising'}
WHERE name = 'Tom Clancy';
```

Cassandra also supports removing items from a set using the UPDATE statement:

```
UPDATE authors
SET books = books - {'Red Storm Rising'}
WHERE name = 'Tom Clancy';
```

At the storage layer, set values are stored as column names, with the values left blank. This guarantees uniqueness, as any attempt to rewrite the same item would simply result in overwriting the old column name. The storage representation of the books set would look like this:

```
RowKey: Tom Clancy
=> (name=books:50617472696f742047616d6573, value=)
=> (name=books:576974686f75742052656d6f727365, value=)
        ↑                    ↑
    set name        item (in byte representation)
```

You can see that the name of the set is stored as the first component of the composite column name, with the item as the second component. Sets can be quite useful as a container for unique items in a variety of data models.

Lists

At the CQL level, lists look very similar to sets. In the following table, we substitute the set of books from the previous example for a list:

```
CREATE TABLE authors (
    name text,
    books list<text>,
    PRIMARY KEY (name)
);
```

Insertion is also similar to the set syntax, except that the curly braces are traded for brackets:

```
INSERT INTO authors (name, books)
VALUES ('Tom Clancy', ['Without Remorse', 'Patriot Games']);
```

And since lists are ordered, CQL supports prepend and append operations, which involve simply placing the item as either the first (prepend) or second (append) operands, as follows:

```
UPDATE authors
SET books = books + ['Red Storm Rising']
WHERE name = 'Tom Clancy';

UPDATE authors
SET books = ['Red Storm Rising'] + books
WHERE name = 'Tom Clancy';
```

To delete an item, you can refer to it by name:

```
UPDATE authors
SET books = books - ['Red Storm Rising']
WHERE name = 'Tom Clancy';
```

Unlike set, the list structure at the storage layer places the list item in the column value, and the column name instead contains a UUID for ordering purposes. Here's what it looks like:

```
Row Key: Tom Clancy
=> (name=books:d36de8b0305011e4a0dddbbeade718be, value=576974686f)
=> (name=books:d36de8b1305011e4a0dddbbeade718be, value=506174726)
```

Maps

Lastly, maps are a highly useful structure, as they can offer similar flexibility to the old dynamic column names many grew accustomed to in the Thrift days, as long as the total number of columns is kept to a reasonable number. Just remember that many of the models that used dynamic columns in Thrift (such as time series data) should make use of clustering columns. Maps, on the other hand, can be helpful for cases where some fields may be unknown up front.

For example, we can use a map to store not only the book title but also the year. Here is what that would look like:

```
CREATE TABLE authors (
    name text,
    books map<text, int>,
    PRIMARY KEY (name)
);
```

To insert or update an entire map, use the following syntax:

```
INSERT INTO authors (name, books)
VALUES ('Tom Clancy', {'Without Remorse':1993, 'Patriot Games':1987});
```

You can also insert or update a single key using array-like syntax, as follows:

```
UPDATE authors
SET books['Red Storm Rising'] = 1986
WHERE name = 'Tom Clancy';
```

Specific values can be also be removed by using a DELETE statement:

```
DELETE books['Red Storm Rising']
FROM authors WHERE name = 'Tom Clancy';
```

At the storage layer, maps look very similar to lists, except that the ordering ID is replaced by the map key:

```
RowKey: Tom Clancy
=> (name=books:50617472696f742047616d6573, value=000007c3)
=> (name=books:576974686f75742052656d6f727365, value=000007c9)
```

As you can see, all of these collection types make use of composite columns in the same manner as clustering columns. However, keep in mind that there is currently no range query functionality for collections, so in many cases clustering columns will be a better choice.

Denormalizing with materialized views

There are times when your use case requires you to read data using an alternate key entirely. In order to be able to read your data by partition key, and in sorted order, it is often necessary to write data in more than one way. Prior to version 3.0, we would accomplish this by literally creating and writing to multiple tables, one for each query type.

Fortunately Cassandra now provides an alternative, called **materialized views**. This new feature handles the administrative task of populating these alternate table views, removing the burden from our application and reducing the risk of orphaned data.

Creating a materialized view is straightforward. As an example, let's say we need to query for all authors in a given year, which is not possible with the `authors` table introduced earlier. To accomplish this, we need a view that specifies a primary key starting with the `year` column, followed by clustering columns for both `name` and `title`:

```
CREATE MATERIALIZED VIEW books_by_year AS
  SELECT *
  FROM authors
  WHERE year IS NOT NULL
    AND name IS NOT NULL
    AND title IS NOT NULL
  PRIMARY KEY (year, name, title);
```

As we insert new data into the `authors` table, Cassandra will keep this view up to date, allowing us to run queries such as the following:

```
SELECT * FROM books_by_year
WHERE year = 1987;
```

You'll notice that CQL requires us to specify a non-null query predicate for each of the primary key columns. In the previous example we simply used the `IS NOT NULL` qualifier, but it is also possible to filter data using the `WHERE` clause, similarly to any other CQL statement. Suppose, for instance, that we would like a view consisting solely of books written by a single author. We could do this as follows:

```
CREATE MATERIALIZED VIEW clancy_books AS
  SELECT *
  FROM authors
  WHERE name = 'Tom Clancy'
    AND title IS NOT NULL
    AND year IS NOT NULL
  PRIMARY KEY (name, title, year);
```

There are implications whenever data is modified, as Cassandra must now perform writes to both the base table and the view table(s). However, without this feature, we would need to execute multiple updates from our application, which may be less performant than allowing the database to handle this for us. Additionally, updates to views are atomic, so there is no concern about data getting out of sync.

At this point you should have a good understanding of the building blocks for a solid Cassandra data model. While every use case is different, there are some general themes we can examine to help you think through your own unique model. So let us now have a look at some of these common patterns, beginning with what's likely the most common use of Cassandra: **time series data**.

Working with time series data

For most of the last two decades, data modeling has centered around the *relationships* among various entities. A person has one account but one or many phone numbers. That same person has one or more addresses (such as a home and work address). A person can belong to one or more groups, which can in turn contain many people.

nge over time.

We modeled these relationships using foreign keys and join tables, and we built queries by joining multiple tables together to produce the desired result. But in recent years we have begun to introduce another dimension to our data: time. Now we're interested in more than just how entities are connected, but also how their relationships change over time.

For example, while we previously were concerned only about a set of fixed locations associated with a person, we now have mobile phones with GPS radios in pockets and purses all over the world. This makes it possible to produce a timeline of a person's movements, marrying time and location.

Introducing time into the equation causes significant challenges for a traditional relational database, because it dramatically increases the volume and velocity of data, putting a strain on the monolithic model. Fortunately Cassandra is perfectly suited for this sort of data.

Designing for immutability

An interesting and important difference between modeling relationships versus modeling time series data, is that relational data tends to be mutable whereas time series data is generally immutable. Mutable data is unstable, because it may change at any moment. This makes it more complicated to guarantee that we have the most up-to-date version. Immutable data, by contrast, is stable, which means we can avoid many of the complexities associated with data that can change over time.

 If you find yourself struggling with modeling a particular problem in Cassandra, consider reimagining the model as immutable time series data. This strategy often results in an obvious solution to what appeared to be an intractable problem.

Immutability is a desirable property in a Cassandra data model, as updates and deletes can add complexity related to consistency and performance (remember that SSTables are immutable). Often the easiest way to guarantee immutability is to simply add a time component to your data model. Let's take a look at how we can do this.

Modeling sensor data

We'll start with a ubiquitous use case: sensor data. Sensor readings are inherently time-oriented, and our world is filled with all manner of sensors. As with any Cassandra data model, the first order of business is to examine our intended query patterns.

The queries

For this use case, given a specific sensor, we want to be able to answer two primary questions in real time:

1. What is the current sensor reading?
2. What were the readings between time x and time y?

To answer the first question, our model must allow us to retrieve only the latest value, so we know we must order the data by a timestamp. Since the data will be ordered by time, we should also be able to support the second query, as it involves selecting a range of times. As we learned earlier in this chapter, Cassandra does well with ranges based on sort order.

Time-based ordering

We have established that we must know the partition key at query time, and that the key must distribute well across the cluster. Since we're going to look up the data by sensorID, one option might be to use this ID as the partition key. We can then store the timestamp as a clustering column in order to get time-based ordering. Here's what that model would look like:

```
CREATE TABLE sensor_readings (
    sensorID uuid,
    timestamp bigint,
    reading decimal,
    PRIMARY KEY (sensorID, timestamp)
) WITH CLUSTERING ORDER BY (timestamp DESC);
```

If you consider our earlier discussion on how this type of model translates to the storage layer, it should be clear that this could be problematic. If we presume that sensors will continue to collect data indefinitely, the result of this data model will be unbounded row growth. This is because each new CQL row for a given sensor is actually adding columns to the same storage row. Eventually this model will result in an unsustainable number of columns in each row, with no easy way to archive off old data. It would be tempting to resolve this by simply deleting a range of values at the end of the partition, but this is actually an anti-pattern. See the next chapter for more details on why this is a bad idea.

Using a sentinel value

There is a simple way to address this. We can add a time bucket to the partition key, such that the key is comprised of both the sensorID and the time bucket, where the time bucket is a timestamp rounded to some interval. This gives us a known, time-based value to use as a means of further partitioning our data, and also allows us to easily find keys that can be safely archived. The time bucket is an example of a **sentinel**, and is a useful construct in a number of models where you need better distribution than your natural key provides.

With this in mind, here is a modification of the sensor_readings table:

```
CREATE TABLE sensor_readings (
    sensorID uuid,
    time_bucket int,
    timestamp bigint,
    reading decimal,
    PRIMARY KEY ((sensorID, time_bucket), timestamp)
) WITH CLUSTERING ORDER BY (timestamp DESC);
```

When choosing values for your time buckets, a rule of thumb is to select an interval that allows you to perform the bulk of your queries using only two buckets. The more buckets you query, the more nodes will be involved to produce your result. For more information on this, see Chapter 8, *Anti-Patterns*. It's also worth noting that this would be an excellent time to use time-window compaction.

Satisfying our queries

So the question remains: how does this model allow us to perform the two queries we said were required for our use case? Well, we have seen that we can ask for the data for a specific sensor, as the time bucket can be computed at query time. To do this, we compute a time_bucket that corresponds to the current timestamp rounded down to the start of the time interval.

We can then obtain the latest reading as follows:

```
SELECT * FROM sensor_readings
WHERE sensorID = 53755080-4676-11e4-916c-0800200c9a66
AND time_bucket = 1411840800 LIMIT 1;
```

For the second query, we want a range from time *x* to time *y* for a given sensor. Since our timestamp is a clustering column, this is also possible:

```
SELECT * FROM sensor_readings
WHERE sensorID = 53755080-4676-11e4-916c-0800200c9a66
AND time_bucket IN (1411840800, 1411844400)
AND timestamp >= 1411841700
AND timestamp <= 1411845300;
```

Thus, we have answered both our queries with a model that scales and performs well, and that doesn't require a large number of nodes to participate. This time series model should form the basis of many of your use cases, whether they initially appear to be time series data or not.

When time is all that matters

In the previous example, we were looking for time-ordered data for a given object, in this case a sensor. But there are cases when what we really need is to simply get a list of the latest readings from all sensors. We need a different model to address this, because our previous model required that we know which sensor we were querying.

It would be tempting to simply remove `sensorID` from the primary key, using only `time_bucket` as the partition key. The problem with this strategy is that all writes and most reads would be against a single partition key. This would create a single hotspot that would move around the cluster as the interval changed. Keep in mind that a materialized view would result in the same problem, since the view itself would contain hotspots.

As a result, it is imperative that you determine some sentinel value that can be used in place of the `sensorID`, and that is not time oriented. For example, sensor type or a hash of the `sensorID` could be a good value. In practice I have found that this use case is rare, or that the real use case requires a queue or cache. Using Cassandra, or most databases for that matter, as a queue is an antipattern. You can read more about this and other antipatterns in `Chapter 8`, *Anti-Patterns*.

Understanding how to model time series data is an essential skill that you will employ over and over again as you work with various types of data in Cassandra. When in doubt about how to model a given use case, start by viewing it as time series data. You will find that the model fits more often than not.

Working with geospatial data

Another very common use of Cassandra is to store and query geospatial data. Typically the objective with this type of data is to find points near a given location. The challenge is to find a key that can be used to narrow down the potential list of locations, and to avoid querying many keys at once.

While there is more than one possible data structure that can be used for this purpose, geohashing has a number of benefits that make it worth considering. A geohash is a base-32 representation of a geographic area, where each additional digit represents greater precision. The property of geohashes that makes them particularly suited for geospatial searches is that adding a level of precision to a given geohash results in an area contained within the lower-precision value.

We can visualize this using the following diagram, which shows a geohash, dnh03, with a number of more precise geohashes contained within it. All of the smaller geohashes begins with the dnh03 prefix:

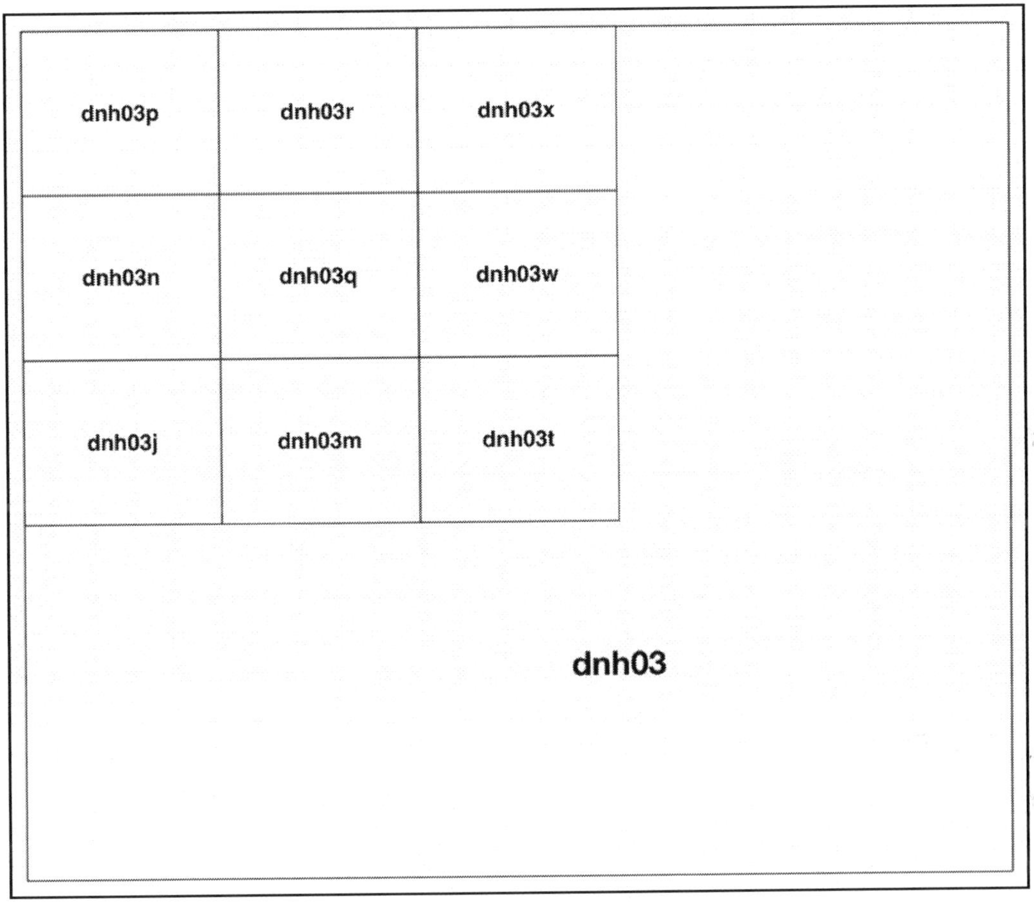

Essentially, geohashes represent the globe as a binary search tree, starting with each hemisphere as the first nodes. One benefit of using this method over other data structures is that there is a single scheme that is universally recognized, similar to using latitude and longitude to represent a point.

To represent searchable data, we can use a low-precision geohash as the partition key, and then the full geohash can be stored as a clustering column. The chosen precision will determine how many keys must be queried to produce results to fill the search space. So our data model would be as follows:

```
CREATE TABLE geo_search (
    geo_key text,
    geohash text,
    place_name text,
    PRIMARY KEY (geo_key, geohash)
);
```

Let's assume we want to store locations with a range of approximately 2.5 km. This translates to a `geo_key` precision of five digits. Using this as our model, an insert would look like this:

```
INSERT INTO geo_search (geo_key, geohash, place_name)
VALUES ('dnh03', 'dnh03pt4', 'Green Grocery Store');
```

If necessary, you can also insert values with keys at multiple precision levels, enabling either coarse- or fine-grained queries. To query for points near a location, you can simply compute the geohash of the location, then truncate it to the precision level of the key. Once you have this value, a simple select produces the desired results.

For example, to find points near Green Grocery Store, use the following query:

```
SELECT * FROM geo_search WHERE geo_key = 'dnh03';
```

Note that `dnh03` is simply the full geohash of Green Grocery Store truncated down to five digits to match the precision of the key. Depending on the search area, it may be necessary to request more than one key. This strategy allows you to model and query geospatial data with minimal cost and overhead across a large Cassandra cluster.

You can also easily imagine combining geohashing with time series data to keep track of location changes over time. This can be accomplished by creating a partition key consisting of time bucket and low-precision geohash. This model allows for querying a range of time for a given location.

While your data model may vary from the two approaches covered here, you will likely find that querying by time and space will be a common use case. This section has prepared you to tackle those data models with confidence.

Summary

In this chapter, we laid down a general foundation for data modeling that should give you the tools you need to correctly reason about your specific use cases. We have covered a lot of ground, including Cassandra's storage engine and how your CQL gets translated to that underlying model, as well as a guide for modeling time series and geospatial data.

But there are also a number of mistakes people make when modeling data for Cassandra, and we will talk about these in the next chapter on antipatterns. Make sure to read on, so that you can avoid these common pitfalls.

8
Anti-Patterns

When working with new or unfamiliar technology, we can find ourselves struggling to apply it to the problem at hand. This is why it is a common practice in software engineering to seek out established design patterns. Such patterns provide guide rails to keep us headed in the right direction, and therefore avoid the traps that await those who try to figure it out on their own.

Design patterns are established through the (often painful) experience of early technology adopters who have blazed the trails and provided us with nicely groomed paths. But with any given technology, we find some commonly used trails leading to dangers in the woods. In software design, we call these **anti-patterns**.

In the last chapter, we focused on how to model your data correctly to take advantage of Cassandra's natural sorting and distribution properties. This chapter, by contrast, will take the opposite approach. We will expose many of the well-worn but dangerous paths so that you can avoid these common pitfalls.

Specifically, we will deal with the following topics:

- Multi-key queries
- Secondary indices
- Distributed joins
- Deletes (and tombstones)
- Unbounded row growth

Those who have been around the block with Cassandra can likely point to a time when they were lured unsuspectingly into at least one of the traps in the previous list. For the benefit of everyone else, let's fully explore each of these topics to help others steer clear of the dangers.

In many ways, this chapter is an extension of the last, as we will be using the same idioms to discuss data models and their representation at the storage layer. If you are unfamiliar with these concepts, it would be advisable to review the last chapter to avoid confusion regarding the terminology.

One common theme with most of the anti-patterns we will discuss is that they often appear to work fine at a smaller scale. But once you grow your dataset or cluster size, you can end up with increased latencies, failing queries, and availability problems. Some of these patterns can be used very carefully under specific circumstances, but you must clearly understand the limitations.

The first pattern we will examine involves a query pattern that results in some non-obvious consequences: **querying by multiple keys**.

Multi-key queries

You will recall from the last chapter that Cassandra is most efficient when querying a range of columns on disk. All our examples assumed a replication factor of 3 with QUORUM reads and writes. We will follow the same conventions with the examples in this chapter.

With this in mind, let's make use of the authors schema we introduced in the last chapter:

```
CREATE TABLE authors (
    name text,
    year int,
    title text,
    publisher text,
    isbn text,
    PRIMARY KEY (name, year, title)
);
```

Using this schema, let's say we want to retrieve a number of books from a list of known authors. Obviously, we could write a separate query for each author, but Cassandra also provides a familiar SQL-style syntax for specifying multiple partition keys using the IN clause:

```
SELECT * FROM authors
WHERE name IN (
    'Tom Clancy',
    'Malcolm Gladwell',
    'Dean Koontz'
);
```

The question is: how will Cassandra fulfill this request? As we have discussed numerous times throughout this book, the system will hash the partition keyâ⊚⊚name in this case-and assign replicas to nodes based on the hash. Using the three authors in our query as examples, we will end up with a distribution resembling the following:

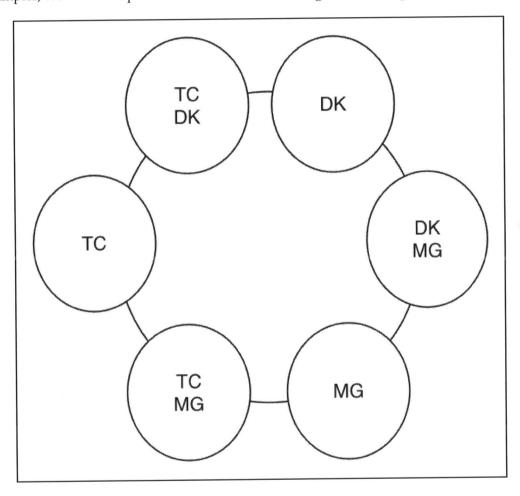

The distribution of keys across a six-node cluster using a replication factor of 3

The important characteristic to note in this distribution is that the keys are dispersed randomly throughout the cluster. If we also remember that a QUORUM read requires consulting with at least two out of three replicas, it is easy to see how this query will result in consulting many nodes. In the following diagram, our client makes a request to one of the nodes, which will act as coordinator. The coordinator must then make requests to at least two replicas for each key in the query:

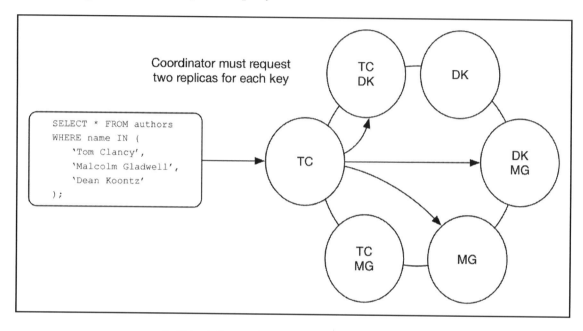

The IN clause in this query results in consulting four total nodes to satisfy the query

The end result is that we require four out of six nodes to fulfill this query! If any one of these calls fails, the entire query will fail. It is easy to see how a query with many keys could require participation from every node in the cluster.

When using the IN clause, it's best to keep the number of keys small. There are valid use cases for this clause, such as querying across time buckets for time series models, but in such cases, you should try to size your buckets such that you only need at most two in order to fulfill the request.

In fact, it is often advisable to issue multiple queries in parallel as opposed to utilizing the IN clause. While the IN clause may save you from multiple network requests to Cassandra, the coordinator must do more work. You can often reduce overall latency and workload with several token-aware queries (see Chapter 6, *High Availability Features in the Native Java Client* for details on this concept), as you'll be talking directly to the nodes that contain the data.

There is an additional benefit in running separate queries rather than a single multi-key query. When using the IN clause, if any one key times out, you will have to retry the entire query. On the other hand, using separate queries allows you to retry only the query that timed out.

Secondary indices

If range queries can be considered optimal for Cassandra's storage engine, queries based on a **secondary index** fall at the other end of the spectrum. Secondary indices have been a part of Cassandra since the 0.7 release, and they are certainly an alluring feature. In fact, for those who are accustomed to modeling data in relational databases, creating an index is often a go-to strategy to achieve better query performance. However, as with most aspects of the transition to Cassandra, this strategy translates poorly.

To start, let's get familiar with what secondary indices are and how they work. The purpose of an index is to allow **query-by-value** functionality, which is not supported naturally. This should be a clue as to the potential danger involved in relying on the index functionality.

As an example, suppose we want to be able to query authors for a given publisher. Using out earlier authors table, remember that the publisher column has no special properties. It is a simple text column, meaning that by default we cannot filter based on its value. We can take a look at what happens when attempting to do so, as in the following query:

```
SELECT * FROM authors
WHERE publisher = 'Putnam';
```

Running this query results in the following error message, indicating that we're trying to query by the value of a non-indexed column:

```
InvalidRequest: code=2200 [Invalid query] message="Cannot execute this
query as it might involve data filtering and thus may have unpredictable
performance. If you want to execute this query despite the performance
unpredictability, use ALLOW FILTERING"
```

The error message gives a hint about why this functionality is unnatural. Because we have not specified the partition key, this query will require a full, distributed table scan. The seemingly obvious remedy is to simply create an index on `publisher`, as follows:

```
CREATE INDEX authors_publisher
ON authors (publisher);
```

Now we can filter on `publisher`, so our problems are solved, right? Not exactly! Let's look closely at what Cassandra does to make this work.

Secondary indices under the hood

At the storage layer, a secondary index is simply another table, where the key is the value of the indexed column, and the columns contain the row keys of the indexed table. This can be a bit confusing to describe, so let's visualize it.

Imagine our `authors` table contains the following CQL rows:

Name	Year	Title	Publisher
Tom Clancy	1987	Patriot Games	Putnam
Dean Koontz	1991	Cold Fire	Headline
Anne Rice	1998	Pandora	Random House
Charles Dickens	1838	Oliver Twist	Random House

An index on `publisher` would then look like this at the storage layer:

```
Row Key: Putnam
=> (name=Tom Clancy, value=)

Row Key: Headline
=> (name=Dean Koontz, value=)

Row Key: Random House
=> (name=Anne Rice, value=)
=> (name=Charles Dickens, value=)
```

So a query filtering on `publisher` will use the index to each author `name`, and then query all the authors by key. This is similar to using the `IN` clause, since we must query replicas for every key with an entry in the index.

But it's actually even worse than the `IN` clause, because of a very important difference between indices and standard tables. Cassandra co-locates index entries with their associated original table keys. In other words, you will end up with a key for Random House in `author_publishers` on every node that has keys for Anne Rice or Charles Dickens in `authors`.

To make this a bit clearer, the following diagram shows how our co-located `authors` table and `author_publisher` index might be distributed across a four-node cluster:

Node 1

Authors
"Tom Clancy" : "Putnam"
"Anne Rice" : "Random House"
"Dean Koontz" : "Headline"

Index
"Putnam" : "Tom Clancy"
"Random House" : "Anne Rice"
"Headline" : "Dean Koontz"

Node 2

Authors
"Tom Clancy" : "Putnam"
"Charles Dickens" : "Random House"
"Anne Rice" : "Random House"

Index
"Putnam" : "Tom Clancy"
"Random House" : "Anne Rice",
            "Charles Dickens"

Node 3

Authors
"Charles Dickens" : "Random House"
"Anne Rice" : "Random House"
"Dean Koontz" : "Headline"

Index
"Random House" : "Anne Rice",
            "Charles Dickens"
"Headline" : "Dean Koontz"

Node 4

Authors
"Tom Clancy" : "Putnam"
"Dean Koontz" : "Headline"
"Charles Dickens" : "Random House"

Index
"Putnam" : "Tom Clancy"
"Headline" : "Dean Koontz"
"Random House" : "Charles Dickens"

Index entries are located on the node where the indexed key is stored

The objective of using this approach is to be able to determine which nodes own indexed keys, as well as to obtain the keys themselves in a single request. But the problem is that we have no idea which token ranges contain indexed keys until we ask each range. So now we end up with a query pattern like this:

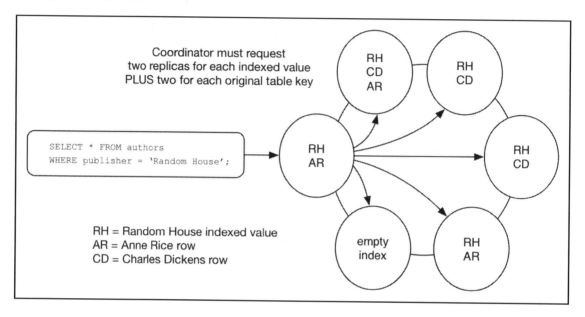

A secondary index query requires consulting with all nodes in the cluster

Obviously, the use of secondary indices has an enormous impact on both performance and availability, since all nodes must participate in fulfilling the query. While this could be acceptable for occasional queries, trying to do it with critical, high-volume queries will be problematic. In a distributed system with many nodes, there is a high likelihood that at least one node will be unable to respond. For this reason, it's best to avoid using them in favor of materialized views or another data model entirely.

If you decide to use a secondary index for a use case where performance and availability are not critical, make sure you only index on low-cardinality values, as high-cardinality indices do not scale well. But don't go so low that your index is rendered useless. For example, booleans are bad, as are UUIDs, but birth year could be a reasonable column to index.

Often you will find that your chosen data model does not satisfy all your queries. If this is the case, you should leverage materialized views to support the additional queries (see Chapter 7, *Modeling for Availability* for more details).

Improvements with SASI

One of the problems with the traditional index mechanism is that it requires two passes through the read path on each node, one to read the index and one to read the data. This double-pass introduces significant latency and unnecessary load on the system. As of version 3.4, there is another option called an **SSTable Attached Secondary Index (SASI)**.

SASI indices offer improvements in performance, resource utilization, and functionality. The key innovation that enables these enhancements is that—as the name implies—the index is attached to the SSTable itself, rather than being relegated to a separate table. This means the read path is much more straightforward, requiring only a single pass to read both the index and the underlying data.

Creating a SASI index is straightforward, but there are many options available to enable a variety of query predicates. To enable retrieving authors by publisher as in our previous example (using the default options), you can issue the following statement:

```
CREATE CUSTOM INDEX authors_publisher
ON authors(publisher)
USING 'org.apache.cassandra.index.sasi.SASIIndex';
```

For more information on the various options available for SASI indices, check out the full documentation at https://docs.datastax.com/en/cql/3.3/cql/cql_reference/refCreateSASIIndex.html.

But be aware that SASI indices still follow the same query pattern as traditional indices, and therefore you should use them with caution for applications where performance and availability are critical. Interestingly, secondary indices are actually one form of a more general anti-pattern that's just as common. Let's take a look at this concept now.

Distributed joins

With relational databases, we write different data entities in their own tables, and then we join them to form the desired view at query time. If we apply this idea to a database like Cassandra, we end up with a distributed join.

New Cassandra developers, especially those who come from a relational database background, are particularly prone to following this pattern. In the last chapter, we mentioned that denormalization is the key to successful data modeling in Cassandra, and our discussion of secondary indices can help explain the reasons for this.

If you find yourself querying multiple large tables and then joining them in your application based on some shared key, you are performing a distributed join. This should almost always be avoided in favor of a denormalized data model. The only exception is for very small lookup tables that can fit easily in memory. Otherwise, you should always write your data the way you intend to read it.

At this point, you should be familiar enough with distributed join patterns to know why they should be avoided, so it's time to move on to another common source of problems in Cassandra: deletes.

Deleting data

We have established that Cassandra employs a log-structured storage engine, where all writes are immutable appends to the log. The implication is that data cannot actually be deleted at the time a DELETE statement is issued. Cassandra solves this by writing a marker, called a **tombstone**, with a timestamp greater than the previous value. This has the effect of overwriting the previous value with an empty one, which will then be compiled in subsequent queries for that column in the same manner as any other update.

Garbage collection

Eventually, these tombstones are reconciled with earlier values as part of the compaction process, where the earlier values are discarded. See Chapter 7, *Modeling for Availability* for more details on how compaction works. There are two possibilities for when data can be physically deleted and tombstones collected.

If a delete occurs while the data is still in the memtable (and therefore, not yet flushed to disk), the existing data will be immediately replaced by the tombstone. Otherwise, the tombstone is simply written to the memtable. In either case, it will eventually get flushed to disk, where it will continue to live until it is garbage-collected.

For a tombstone to be deleted, two events must occur. First, the age of the tombstone must exceed the value of `gc_grace_seconds`, as specified in `cassandra.yaml`. Once this time has elapsed, the next compaction to run on the SSTable containing the tombstone will cause it to be purged as long as the compaction includes all SSTables covered by the tombstone.

Resurrecting the dead

An astute observer may have noticed a potential problem with tombstones in an eventually consistent system. Let's assume that multiple replicas exist for a given column, yet only one has recorded the tombstone. If one of the nodes remains down past `gc_grace_seconds` without a repair operation, when it finally comes back online, it will still contain the old data and be unaware of the delete. Any subsequent repair will then recreate the old data on other nodes as if the delete had never occurred.

> TIP
>
> To ensure that deleted data never resurfaces, make sure you run repair at least once every `gc_grace_seconds`, and never let a node stay down for longer than this time period.

The problem with tombstones

You may be wondering why we've spent so much time discussing tombstones in a chapter on anti-patterns. The last example should provide a hint to the reason. When a query requires reading tombstones, Cassandra must perform many reads to return your results. Depending on your data model, this could result in thousands of tombstones read for a given partition!

In addition, a query for a key in an SSTable that has only tombstones associated with it will still pass through the bloom filter, because the system must reconcile tombstones with other replicas. The bloom filter is a data structure that's designed to prevent unnecessary reads for missing data, but in this case there is actual data to be read. So Cassandra must perform extra reads even after data has been deleted.

Now that you understand the basics of deletes and the problems associated with them, it's important to point out the other ways deletes can be generatedâ©©sometimes in ways you would not expect.

Expiring columns

Cassandra offers us a handy feature for purging old data through setting an expiration time, called a **TTL**, at the column level. There are many valid reasons to set TTL values, and they can help avoid unbounded data accumulation over time. Setting a TTL on a column is straightforward, and can be accomplished using either an INSERT or UPDATE statement as follows (note that TTL values are in seconds):

```
INSERT INTO authors (name, title, year)
VALUES ('Tom Clancy', 'Patriot Games', 1987)
USING TTL 86400;

UPDATE authors USING TTL 86400
SET publisher = 'Putnam'
WHERE name = 'Tom Clancy'
AND title = 'Patriot Games'
AND year = 1987;
```

This can be useful when dealing with ephemeral data, but you must take care while employing this strategy, because an expired column results in a tombstone as in any other form of delete.

TTL anti-patterns

A common reason to expire columns is in the case of time series data. Imagine we want to display a feed of comments associated with a news article, where the newest post appears at the top. To avoid holding onto them indefinitely, we set them to expire after a few hours.

So we end up with a model that resembles the following:

```
CREATE TABLE comments (
    articleID uuid,
    timestamp int,
    username text,
    comment text,
    PRIMARY KEY (articleID, timestamp, username)
) WITH CLUSTERING ORDER BY (timestamp DESC);
```

We then insert new comments with a three-hour TTL:

```
INSERT INTO comments (articleID, timestamp, username, comment)
VALUES (36f08b19-fc6d-4930-81f6-6704f627ca83,
        1413146590, 'rs_atl', 'Nice article!')
USING TTL 10800;
```

It's important to note that this model is perfectly acceptable so far. Where we can run into problems is when we naively attempt to query for the latest values. It can be tempting to assume that we can simply query everything for a given articleID, with the expectation that old columns will simply disappear. In other words, we perform a query like this:

```
SELECT * FROM comments
WHERE articleID = 36f08b19-fc6d-4930-81f6-6704f627ca83;
```

In some ways this expectation is correct. Old values will disappear from the result set, and for a period of time this query will perform perfectly well. But we will gradually accumulate tombstones as columns reach their expiration time, and this query requires that we read all columns in the storage row. Eventually, we will reach a point where Cassandra will be reading more tombstones than real values!

The solution is simple. We must add a range filter on timestamp, which will tell Cassandra to stop scanning columns at approximately as far back in time as the tombstones will start. In this case, we don't want to read any columns older than 3 hours, so our new query looks like this:

```
SELECT * FROM comments
WHERE articleID = 36f08b19-fc6d-4930-81f6-6704f627ca83
AND timestamp > [current_time - 10800];
```

Note that you will have to calculate the timestamp in your application, as CQL does not currently support arithmetic operations.

To sum up, expiring columns can be highly useful as long as you do so wisely. Make sure your usage pattern avoids reading excessive numbers of tombstones. Often you can use range filters to accomplish this goal. Adding a row limit using the LIMIT clause can help to ensure that you don't inadvertently return a large number of rows. Also, these models are a good fit for the new time-window compaction strategy, as it's optimized for the efficient collection of TTL'ed data.

When null does not mean empty

There is an even subtler (and more insidious) way to inadvertently create tombstones: by inserting nullvalues. Let's see how we might cause this situation unwittingly.

We know that Cassandra stores columns sparsely, meaning that unspecified values simply aren't written. So it would seem logical that setting a column to `null` would result in a missing column. In fact, writing a `null` is the same thing as explicitly deleting a column, and therefore a tombstone is written for that column!

There is a simple reason why this is the case. While Cassandra supports separate `INSERT` and `UPDATE` statements, all writes are fundamentally the same under the covers. And because all writes are simply append operations, there is no way for the system to know whether a previous value exists for the column. Therefore Cassandra must actually write a tombstone in order to guarantee any old values are deleted.

While it may seem as though this would be easy to avoidâ◎◎by just not writing null valuesâ◎◎it is fairly easy to mistakenly allow this to happen when using prepared statements. Imagine a data model that includes many sparsely populated columns. It is tempting to create a single prepared statement with all potential columns, then set the unused columns to `null`. It is also possible that callers of an insert method might pass in `null` values. If this condition is not checked, it is easy to see how tombstones could be accumulated without realizing this is happening.

Perhaps the subtlest means by which `null` values are introduced is through collections. Any time a collection is deleted or updated, you can end up inserting `null`. Be wary of write patterns that do this frequently.

Fortunately, version 4 of the native protocol (support starting from version 3.0 of the driver) helps to address this issue by allowing you to leave some parameters of a prepared statement unbound. However, you must still ensure that you aren't passing in `null` values.

To wrap up our discussion of deletes, let's look at a common anti-pattern involving deletes.

Cassandra is not a queue

The idea of using a database as a durable queue is certainly not a new one. For many years, people have been misappropriating relational databases for use as queues. On the surface, it may seem that Cassandra would work well as a distributed durable queue, as it easily supports querying based on insertion order. Here is an example data model that would serve this use case:

```
CREATE TABLE queue (
    name text,
    timestamp int,
    item text,
    PRIMARY KEY (name, timestamp)
);
```

We could then support an enqueue operation with a simple insert, perhaps including an expiration time to avoid holding onto irrelevant items:

```
INSERT INTO queue (name, timestamp, item)
VALUES ('to_do', 1413146590, 'Learn Scala');
```

And a dequeue operation would involve querying the first (which equates to the oldest in this case) item, and then deleting it:

```
SELECT * FROM queue
WHERE name = 'to_do'
ORDER BY timestamp ASC LIMIT 1;

DELETE FROM queue
WHERE name = 'to_do'
AND timestamp = [timestamp_of_dequeued_item];
```

Based on our discussion of deletes and tombstones, it should be obvious that we'll be creating three tombstones for every dequeue operation (one for the marker column and one for each non-clustering column). While this may seem similar to the earlier example where we were constantly reading and deleting comments, there is an important distinction.

In the article comments model, we were reading from one end of the range (the latest comments) and deleting from the other end (the earliest comments). This allowed us to scan from the head of the range without the risk of reading any tombstones, and simply apply a range filter to make sure we never read so far that we encounter any at the other end. With the queue model, we are doing the opposite: we are reading and deleting from the same end of the range. The result, over time, looks like this:

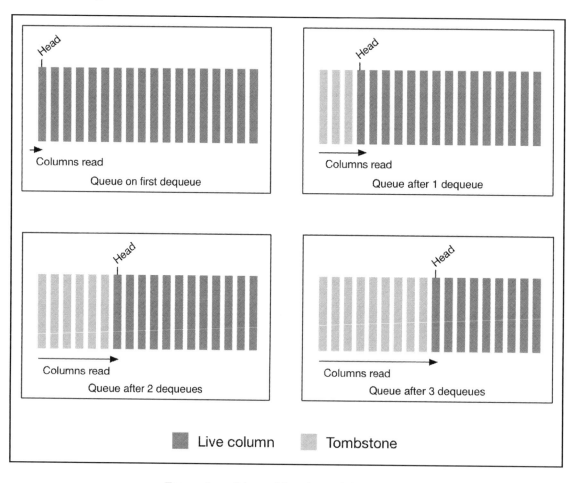

The queue pattern results in accumulating tombstones at the head of the range

As you can see from the diagram, with each dequeue operation, three tombstones (the marker plus clustering columns) are added to the head of the queue. Then, when we run a query to obtain the actual head, we must scan through all of these tombstones before reaching it. Obviously, this is not a sustainable strategy, which is why the queue is an anti-pattern.

When building your data models, beware of strategies that are actually queues masquerading as something else. In general, it's important to avoid data structures where you must perform many deletes on a range of data you will frequently read. With large datasets, you can end up reading more tombstones than actual values, and your application may grind to a halt.

To sum up, remember that databases typically make poor queues. If you need a queue, choose a system that was designed to support that use case. There are a number of excellent distributed queues available, so avoid the temptation to use Cassandra for this purpose.

Also, this is a good time to offer a reminder of the advice given in the last chapter to write data immutably. If you avoid deletes where possible, many of the issues from this section can be avoided naturally.

Unbounded row growth

Now let us take a look at the counterpoint problem to deletes, when data for a given key grows without bounds. This is a surprisingly easy situation to get yourself into, especially if you do not understand how Cassandra stores your data on disk. Perhaps the best antidote to unbounded row growth is to read and understand the previous chapter, which offers the foundational knowledge to help you avoid this scenario.

To clarify, this section is not a warning against unbounded growth of your data set in general. We have established that Cassandra scales linearly, so you can continue to add data as long as you have capacity in your cluster. Instead, we are referring to a model where a given partition key continues to accumulate columns with no end in sight. We briefly touched on this in Chapter 7, *Modeling for Availability*, but the topic deserves full treatment.

We can imagine a typical scenario using the `sensor_readings` data model described in the last chapter. Here is a reminder of what it looks like:

```
CREATE TABLE sensor_readings (
    sensorID uuid,
    timestamp int,
    reading decimal,
    PRIMARY KEY (sensorID, timestamp)
);
```

There are two fundamental problems with this model:

- Data will be collected for a given sensor indefinitely, and in many cases at very high frequency.
- With `sensorID` as the partition key, the row will grow by two columns for every reading (one marker and one reading).

It should be noted that this is not actually a problem in terms of queries, provided that they are limited either by a row count or a reasonable range filter on `timestamp`. Instead, you should recall from Chapter 2, *Data Distribution* that the unit of distribution across the cluster is the partition key, in this case, `sensorID`. It is therefore possible with this model that a single key might become so large that it could outgrow a single node! Each Cassandra partition can support a maximum of two billion columns, but in practice the number should be much lessâ⊙⊙with the important point that partitions should have as even a distribution as possible.

For this reason, it is important to choose a reasonable partition key that will prevent unbounded row growth. For time series data, this typically means adding a time bucket to the partition key as described in the time series section in the last chapter. In fact, most models with the potential to suffer from this problem will be time-based, so the bucketing solution is typically the best strategy to avoid the situation. For more information on how to detect wide row problems, refer to Chapter 9, *Failing Gracefully.*

Summary

In this chapter, we discussed some common data modeling patterns to avoid. But it would be impossible to cover every bad choice a user might make, so it's important to focus on understanding the fundamentals of sound design. This will give you a foundation that will allow you to make correct data modeling decisions on whatever problem you may encounter.

As we have also seen in this chapter, sometimes Cassandra isn't the right tool for the problem at hand. Hopefully, you can now recognize when this is the case and choose the right tool for the right job.

It is now time to wrap up this book by taking a look at the ways in which things can go wrong when running Cassandra. While it is a highly fault-tolerant system, you will rest easier if you know what to do when the unexpected happens.

9
Failing Gracefully

Technology organizations, from the CTO to the system administrators, have spent countless hours over the years trying to prevent their database systems from experiencing failure. This is because failure typically meant downtime for the application or, even worse, a loss of critical data.

As we discussed in `Chapter 1`, *Cassandra's Approach to High Availability*, attempts to make these systems highly available often still required a significant amount of human intervention to restore functionality in the event of a failure. Cassandra, as we have learned, was designed from the ground up to consider failure as a normal operational state. This is because in a large distributed system, the chance that at any given moment a piece of hardware will fail is relatively high, so the system must know how to deal with those problems.

But even a robust system like Cassandra, which is designed to handle failure scenarios without losing data or compromising availability, requires vigilance and know-how to keep things running smoothly day in and day out. As we near the end of this book, let's take a moment to examine some of the things that can go bump in the night, and how we might handle those situations. Fortunately, Cassandra provides a number of tools to deal with a great many of the common failure scenarios that can present themselves from time to time.

In this chapter, we will cover the following topics:

- Monitoring Cassandra
- Failure detection
- Logging
- Recovering from node failures
- Backups

Knowledge is power

Of course, the first step in handling anomalous situations is to be aware that something is amiss. As proponents of the Unix philosophy have famously stated, a system must not just function well, but it must also be seen to function well. This is called the **rule of transparency**, and in essence it admonishes application designers to build systems that provide visibility into their inner workings.

Taking this a step further, we might add that we should be able to know that the system is working even when we aren't looking. There are times when you may be actively watching the cluster, for example when adding or removing nodes or deploying a new application. But more often than not, you will have your attention turned elsewhere when the unexpected occurs. It is during these periods that you will need to rely on automated monitoring to alert you that there is trouble.

Monitoring via JMX

Fortunately, Cassandra makes this easy by providing numerous **Java Management Extensions (JMX)** targets that publish all kinds of statistics to give you a window into the state and health of the system. You do not need to know a significant amount about JMX to be able to use it effectively. Essentially, it is a standard mechanism by which applications built on the **Java Virtual Machine (JVM)** can expose metrics and management functions via a common interface.

There are numerous tools for monitoring JMX targets, from the simple JConsole that ships with the **Java Development Kit (JDK),** to sophisticated automated monitoring tools that can alert administrators or even take action based on a set of rules. A simple tool is sufficient for exploring the various targets and learning more about JMX in general, but for production deployments, you will want to make use of an automated tool that can work across your entire cluster.

By default, Cassandra listens for JMX connections on port 7199. To connect to a remote host for monitoring, you will need to configure JMX to allow remote connections. Detailed documentation for accomplishing this can be found on Oracle's website at the following URL:

```
http://docs.oracle.com/javase/8/docs/technotes/guides/management/agent.html
```

Once you have configured your Cassandra hosts to allow remote JMX connections, you can connect using any JMX client. Assuming you have a JDK installation on your local computer, you can connect using JConsole as follows:

First, open a terminal and start JConsole using the `jconsole` command. Then, fill in the host, port, and your credentials in the dialog box, and click on the **Connect** button:

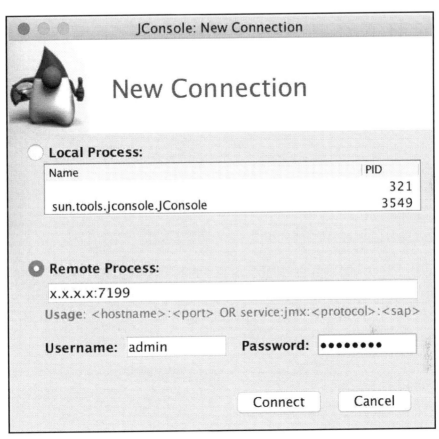

Once JConsole connects to the remote host, you will see an overview of basic statistics for the host, such as memory and CPU utilization. To access the Cassandra-specific information, choose the **MBeans** tab at the top of the window. In this tab, you can see a list of available mbean categories, some of which are provided by default in the JVM; others are specific to the application, in this case, those starting with `org.apache.cassandra`.

If you expand one of the Cassandra categories, this will expose the various objects that can be inspected. Under each object, you can either view attributes or perform operations on the object. For example, if you open the `org.apache.cassandra.db` category and then expand the `Caches` object, you will have access to a variety of statistics, such as hit rates, cache sizes, and the like. You can also perform operations such as clearing row or key caches:

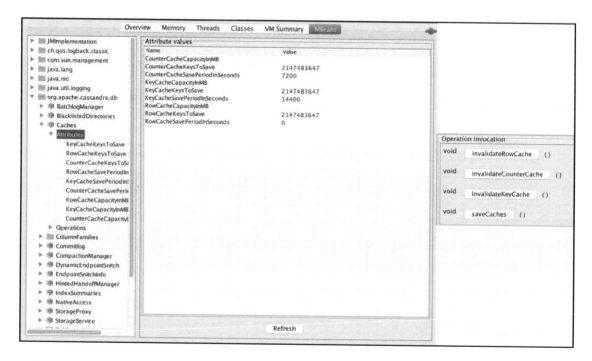

While this may be helpful for working with a local Cassandra instance or exploring the available attributes and operations, JConsole is not a practical tool for managing an entire cluster. A generic, graphical tool such as JConsole can also be unwieldy when trying to perform simple tasks on remote servers. For this reason, Cassandra ships with a useful command-line utility called `nodetool`, which exposes many of the JMX statistics and operations. The full documentation for this utility can be found at `https://docs.datastax` `.com/en/cassandra/3.x/cassandra/tools/toolsNodetool.html`.

Using OpsCenter

DataStax also provides an excellent web-based Cassandra administration tool called OpsCenter that interfaces with JMX to provide a cluster-wide view of your system. It also exposes management functions that allow you to perform system-wide changes without manually editing configuration files or calling JMX functions on every node individually.

To install OpsCenter on your cluster, download the appropriate package from the following URL:

```
http://docs.datastax.com/en/opscenter/5./opsc/install/opscInstallation_g.htm
l
```

OpsCenter offers a variety of useful tools to ease the Cassandra management workload, especially repair, configuration, and topology changes. There are community and enterprise versions of OpsCenter that provide different levels of functionality.

Choosing a management toolset

There is a vast array of third-party products and processes available for managing and monitoring distributed systems, and as such the topic cannot be adequately covered in this book. However, this chapter will offer you an overview of the most important monitoring targets so that you can configure your chosen tool correctly.

When choosing a toolset to manage your cluster, at a minimum, you will need it to be able to perform the following functions:

- **Automatically deploy and configure new nodes**: You will quickly realize the necessity for this as your cluster size grows and the process of scaling out manually becomes cumbersome.
- **Keep your configuration in sync across the nodes**: Specifically, this means managing cluster topology files and each machine's cassandra.yaml configuration and cassandra-env.sh. Open source options such as Chef and Puppet are excellent choices for these kinds of tasks.
- **Perform rolling cluster changes**: Any changes that require a node restart, such as configuration changes or version upgrades, will need to be rolled out to a subset of your nodes at a time.
- **Monitor kernel-level metrics**: These include primarily resource utilization details, such as CPU, disk, and memory at the operating system level. Since Cassandra stores a number of important data structures off-heap, simply monitoring the JVM process itself is not sufficient.

- **Monitor JMX targets**: You will certainly want to know when a key metric falls out of the acceptable range, and many monitoring tools offer this capability. As you become more experienced with Cassandra, you may also want the tool to take action to resolve the problem without human intervention. But at the very least, you need to be aware that something is awry.

For smaller installations, a minimal combination of shell scripts, cron jobs, and a simple JMX monitoring tool may be sufficient. But large clusters will demand higher levels of sophistication in this category. When evaluating tools and procedures for monitoring and managing Cassandra in Amazon EC2, you should consult the Netflix engineering blog (`http://techblog.netflix.com/search/label/Cassandra`) and their GitHub site, as they have contributed significant amounts of their knowledge and tooling to the community.

Logging

In addition to keeping an eye on JMX statistics, there are several levels of log files that should be monitored so that they can be analyzed in case of failure. Ideally, you should be using some sort of log aggregation (such as Flume, FluentD, Splunk, or other similar tools) to make it easier to make sense of logs. Also, aggregation ensures that catastrophic node failures don't prevent you from recovering logs from the problematic hosts, which may be the most important bit of diagnostic data available.

Cassandra logs

Cassandra itself provides two logs, and both are located in the configured logging directory, which is `/var/log/cassandra` by default. The first, `system.log`, is a rolling log of Cassandra's logback output. The second, `output.log`, shows standard out and standard error and is overwritten on startup.

If you are experiencing an issue that warrants lower-level logging than the default `INFO` level, you can adjust the logging level by editing the `logback.xml` file (in the `conf` directory), or by using the nodetool `setlogginglevel` command. This also allows you to set the logging level for a specific subsystem, as in the following example:

```
nodetool setlogginglevel org.apache.cassandra.db DEBUG
```

To obtain more granular logging, change INFO to either DEBUG or TRACE. Trace-level output is extremely verbose, so it is recommended that you first use DEBUG as that level should be sufficient for troubleshooting purposes. Keep in mind that a cluster receiving many thousands of writes per second will generate very verbose logs at DEBUG level, so this should be enabled only for a short period of time to diagnose an issue.

Garbage collector logs

As is the case with any JVM-based application, garbage collection is a significant factor in the performance of Cassandra. In certain classes of problems, where Cassandra did not necessarily fail outright but suffered significant performance issues, having GC logs is a significant aid in determining the underlying cause.

GC logging can be enabled in Cassandra by simply adding a few lines at the end of $CASSANDRA_HOME/conf/cassandra-env.sh:

```
JVM_OPTS="$JVM_OPTS -XX:+PrintGCDetails"
JVM_OPTS="$JVM_OPTS -XX:+PrintGCDateStamps"
JVM_OPTS="$JVM_OPTS -XX:+PrintHeapAtGC"
JVM_OPTS="$JVM_OPTS -XX:+PrintTenuringDistribution"
JVM_OPTS="$JVM_OPTS -XX:+PrintGCApplicationStoppedTime"
JVM_OPTS="$JVM_OPTS -XX:+PrintPromotionFailure"
JVM_OPTS="$JVM_OPTS -Xloggc:/var/log/cassandra/gc-`date +%s`.log"
JVM_OPTS="$JVM_OPTS -Xloggc:/var/log/cassandra/gc.log"
JVM_OPTS="$JVM_OPTS -XX:+UseGCLogFileRotation"
JVM_OPTS="$JVM_OPTS -XX:NumberOfGCLogFiles=10"
JVM_OPTS="$JVM_OPTS -XX:GCLogFileSize=10M"
```

The easiest way to view and understand these logs is to use a viewer designed to parse and make sense of them for you. There are a number of such tools available. If you would like to learn more about how to read and understand GC logs, check out this post on the Oracle site:

```
https://blogs.oracle.com/poonam/entry/understanding_g1_gc_logs
```

In addition to Cassandra and GC logs, you should also make sure you keep detailed application logs to diagnose issues with connections, queries, and other such problems that may display symptoms on the client. The native drivers offer useful information in their logs that may be helpful in determining the cause of a variety of issues.

Monitoring node metrics

Whether you are using JMX monitoring software or the `nodetool` utility, it is important to know what statistics are worth watching. The names and locations of specific attributes can vary depending on the Cassandra version, but the key ideas remain the same.

The objective here is to give you an understanding of the available statistics so that you will know how to choose the proper monitoring targets. We will use `nodetool` for this purpose, as its options tend to be more stable. You should find it straightforward to locate the equivalent JMX mbean.

Thread pools

Cassandra's design employs a **staged event-driven architecture (SEDA),** which essentially comprises of message queues (containing events) feeding into thread pools (or stages). The stages fire off messages to other stages via a messaging service. There are stages for handling a variety of tasks.

Running `nodetool tpstats` provides detailed information about what's happening at each of the stages. A buildup of pending tasks in any of the pools is an indicator that there's something wrong. For example, a lot of pending operations in the mutation stage means that writes are backing up (writes are internally referred to as **mutations).** As a result, it is wise to monitor pending thread pool messages as they can be a leading indicator of potential issues.

The following truncated output of the `nodetool tpstats` command shows what you might see in the case of a backlog of mutations:

```
Pool Name                    Active    Pending      Completed
ReadStage                         0          0        4531423
RequestResponseStage              0          0      109089295
MutationStage                     0      53425       49501952
```

There can be any number of reasons why such a situation may occur, but it is imperative that you become aware of the situation as soon as possible, especially if the symptoms are cluster-wide. If a single node is experiencing this kind of difficulty, it may be an indicator of impending hardware failure or some other situation that would require intervention to remedy.

Table statistics

The `nodetool tablestats` command offers a wealth of data points that provide a complete picture of each table in your schema. You can provide a specific keyspace and table to this command, which helps to limit the verbosity of its output.

When we run this command, we get an output resembling the following:

```
Keyspace: test_keyspace
     Read Count: 383953
     Read Latency: 0.9053452870533634 ms.
     Write Count: 125031
     Write Latency: 0.14220190992633827 ms.
     Pending Tasks: 0
       Table: test
       SSTable count: 2
       Space used (live): 1135025
       Space used (total): 1136661
       Space used by snapshots (total): 0
       Off heap memory used (total): 234245
       SSTable Compression Ratio: 0.916869063329679
       Number of keys (estimate): 12544
       Memtable cell count: 0
       Memtable data size: 0
       Memtable off heap memory used: 0
       Memtable switch count: 10
       Local read count: 383953
       Local read latency: 0.045 ms
       Local write count: 125031
       Local write latency: 0.055 ms
       Pending flushes: 0
       Bloom filter false positives: 0
       Bloom filter false ratio: 0.00000
       Bloom filter space used: 16824
       Bloom filter off heap memory used: 0
       Index summary off heap memory used: 54352
       Compression metadata off heap memory used: 0
       Compacted partition minimum bytes: 43
       Compacted partition maximum bytes: 103
       Compacted partition mean bytes: 50
       Average live cells per slice (last five minutes): 0.0
       Maximum live cells per slice (last five minutes): 0.0
       Average tombstones per slice (last five minutes): 0.0
       Maximum tombstones per slice (last five minutes): 0.0
       Dropped mutations: 0
```

In general, the keyspace-level statistics at the top are not particularly useful, as they are aggregates across all the tables in the keyspace. Instead, pay particular attention to local read and write metrics as well as SSTable count, because these data points can offer insight into issues with specific tables. Often an issue with a single table can expose problems with a data model. For example, if you're using size-tiered compaction, a high SSTable count typically means compaction isn't keeping pace with writes. With leveled compaction, watch for a high count in level 0, which also indicates lagging compaction.

In addition, you should keep an eye on average tombstones per slice, as this will tell you how much of your read workload is being consumed by scanning tombstones. A high number here is a clear indicator of either a problem with your data model or issues with your query patterns. Review `Chapter 8`, *Anti-Patterns* for more information on deletes and tombstones to understand how this can happen and what to do to avoid the situation.

Finding latency outliers

Another useful tool for diagnosing table-specific issues is the `nodetool tablehistograms` command. The basic idea is to provide a histogram of read and write latencies per table. This tool gives additional insights beyond average latencies, which can be deceiving, as they can be skewed by outliers. Using `nodetool tablehistograms` allows you to see those outliers more clearly.

The following is a truncated sample output from the command:

Percentile	SSTables	Write Latency (micros)	Read Latency (micros)
50%	2.00	39.50	36.00
75%	3.00	49.00	55.00
95%	5.00	95.00	82.00
98%	7.00	126.84	110.42
99%	10.00	155.13	123.71
Min	0.00	3.00	3.00
Max	10.00	50772.00	314.00

The statistics generated by `nodetool tablehistograms` are calculated from the last time the command was run, so you will effectively reset the numbers with each run.

Communication metrics

Cassandra provides a useful tool for determining the current state of its communications both with other nodes and with connected clients. The `nodetool netstats` command offers particularly helpful insight into the status of read repair operations, data streaming, and pending client requests.

The following output shows a Cassandra node in a normal state:

```
Mode: NORMAL
Not sending any streams.
Read Repair Statistics:
Attempted: 1
Mismatch (Blocking): 0
Mismatch (Background): 0
Pool Name                Active    Pending    Completed
Large Messages           n/a          0            0
Small Messages           n/a          0            0
Gossip Messages          n/a          0            0
```

During read repair, bootstrapping, and loading from a snapshot, Cassandra exchanges data between nodes via a process called **streaming**. The `netstats` command will display details about which nodes are streaming to and from the requested node. The streaming subsystem associates a specific stream plan to each operation. This plan has a UUID to identify it, which can be observed in this `netstats` snippet:

```
Mode: NORMAL
Bulk Load fdf4cc70-10e9-11e3-bed0-27ba85b87bf8
      /192.168.1.163
            Receiving 3 files, 28437084 bytes total
                /var/lib/cassandra/data/Keyspace1/Standard1
                  /Keyspace1-Standard1-tmp-ja-4-Data.db 9244384/
                    9244384 bytes(100%) received from /192.168.1.163
                    /var/lib/cassandra/data/Keyspace1/Standard1/
                      Keyspace1-Standard1-tmp-ja-5-Data.db
                        9249617/9249617 bytes(100%) received from
                          /192.168.1.163
                      /var/lib/cassandra/data/Keyspace1/Standard1/
                        Keyspace1-Standard1-tmp-ja-6-Data.db
                          5635715/9943083 bytes(56%)
                            received from /192.168.1.163
```

Once you have this ID, you can search through the Cassandra log to find entries related to this stream. This can be very helpful if a stream operation appears to be taking too long or has become stuck.

Thus far we have discussed a variety of ways in which you can monitor and detect failures using the available tooling. But Cassandra also has its own mechanisms for managing failure scenarios. Let us take a moment to look at how these processes help us to sleep well at night, knowing that the system will keep functioning even when things go awry.

When a node goes down

In a cluster of any significant size, nodes are bound to become unresponsive for a variety of reasons. Fortunately, Cassandra has a sophisticated mechanism called the **failure detector** that is designed to determine when this has occurred and then mark the node as down.

Most node failures result from temporary conditions, such as network issues. Therefore, Cassandra assumes that the node will eventually come back online and that permanent cluster changes will be executed explicitly using `nodetool`.

Marking a downed node

Each node keeps track of the state of other nodes in the cluster by means of an accrual failure detector (or phi failure detector). This detector evaluates the health of other nodes based on a sliding window of gossip message arrival times. It computes the statistical distribution of those arrival times per node, thus taking into account the current state of the network rather than using naive thresholds or timeouts.

The ultimate result of the failure detection algorithm is a value called phi, which corresponds to the probability that the next gossip message will be received within a certain amount of time. You can specify the phi value that determines when a node is marked as down by setting the `phi_convict_threshold` configuration value in `cassandra.yaml`.

The default for `phi_convict_threshold` is 8, which should be sufficient for most situations. If you are running in a cloud environment without dedicated network resources, you may consider increasing the value to 12, which takes into account the more contentious network environment. In general, lower values favor earlier detection at the cost of unnecessarily downing a host, while higher values will result in longer detection times but will be less likely to mark a functioning host as down.

Note that there is no master list of downed nodes. Each node manages its own list of the state of its peers. To see the current list of peer states maintained by a given node, use the `nodetool status` command.

Handling a downed node

Once a node has been marked as unreachable, Cassandra will stop sending traffic to that node. However, other nodes will continue to try to reach the downed host periodically to determine whether it has recovered.

During this downtime, any replicas destined for the downed node will be stored as hints on whichever node acted as coordinator for the write, assuming you have enabled hinted handoff (see Chapter 3, *Replication* for more details on how this works). So there will likely be many nodes in the cluster holding hints for the downed node. Assuming the node comes back online before the time window (default 3 hours) set in max_hint_window_in_ms (in cassandra.yaml), the hints will be replayed and the replicas restored.

If the host does not recover before the configured time window has elapsed, the hints will be discarded. In this case, it will be necessary to run nodetool repair on the newly recovered host to restore the lost replicas. Furthermore, it is possible that the downed node itself had stored hints that were never replayed, which is yet another reason to run regular repair operations across your cluster.

In general, it is wise to attempt to restore downed hosts during the hint window if you're using hinted handoff, as this will mitigate potential data loss or consistency issues. If you need to permanently remove a node from the cluster, you should run nodetool decommission on that node so that Cassandra can properly redistribute data and inform other nodes.

Handling slow nodes

Sometimes, a node may not become entirely unresponsive but may be slower than others in the cluster. Cassandra employs a **dynamic snitch** to attempt to steer clear of slower nodes when routing read requests (this doesn't work for writes, since all replicas are always contacted, and then Cassandra simply waits for the consistency level to be satisfied).

When performing a read, the coordinator node only requests the full replica from one node and then asks for checksums from other nodes based on the consistency level. The dynamic snitch algorithm attempts to prefer lower latency nodes when requesting the entire record, thus improving read performance. The algorithm takes into account a variety of factors, including recent performance and whether the node in question is currently undergoing a compaction.

Cassandra has a feature called **rapid read protection**, which helps to prevent slow nodes from causing requests to time out. If a request happens to be routed to a slow node, Cassandra can detect this condition and proactively make the request to another node while waiting for the original node to respond. This allows the client to avoid a timeout if the second request returns within the request timeout period.

This feature (which defaults to a setting of `99percentile`) can be enabled as either a fixed time or as a read latency percentile, as follows:

```
ALTER TABLE authors WITH speculative_retry = '10ms';
```

or

```
ALTER TABLE authors WITH speculative_retry = '99percentile';
```

Keep in mind that rapid read protection only helps when the consistency level is lower than the replication factor. In other words, you cannot expect improvement if you request all replicas. In other cases, however, enabling this feature can substantially improve availability during failure scenarios.

Backing up data

While Cassandra itself goes a long way toward reducing the possibility of data loss, it cannot prevent loss or corruption due to administrative or application-level mistakes. For this reason, it is still advisable to maintain backups of critical tables to allow you to recover to a known good point in the past.

Taking a snapshot

Fundamentally, backing up data in Cassandra involves taking a snapshot of the SSTable for a given keyspace at a moment in time, as it must have all the tables in order to properly recover if needed. You can create a snapshot using `nodetool` as follows:

```
nodetool snapshot [keyspace_name]
```

This will create hardlinks to the current SSTables in that keyspace's `snapshots` directory (located inside the data directory, which is located at `/var/lib/cassandra/data/[keyspace_name]` by default), under a directory named based on the Unix epoch at the time the snapshot is generated. The advantage of this approach is that the hardlink does not require any additional disk space. However, you should be sure to remove old snapshots as they will continue to accumulate if not deleted regularly.

An important point to recognize when using the `nodetool snapshot` command is that this builds a snapshot for the target node only. In order to build a snapshot for the entire cluster, you must run this on every node.

In case it isn't obvious, hardlinking files on the local node does not help you recover lost or corrupted data in the event of a failure. So you will need to have a process to copy the snapshots to an offsite location. With a large database, the size of the data set can discourage frequent backups, so fortunately there is a feature to help alleviate this burden.

Incremental backups

In most cases, there is no need to snapshot an entire keyspace for every backup, as most of the data has already been transferred offsite. If you only want the changes from the last snapshot, you can turn on incremental backups by setting `incremental_backups` to `true` in `cassandra.yaml`. This feature is disabled by default.

You will recall from earlier in this book that SSTables are immutable, and they are flushed to disk periodically as memtables reach a defined threshold. The incremental backup process works by hardlinking each new SSTable as it is flushed to disk, thereby providing a backup that's as up to date as the last flush. The combination of the latest snapshot and any incremental backups created since that snapshot creates the most recent possible picture of the state of the keyspace, making more granular recovery possible.

 Make sure to periodically remove old snapshots and backups, as Cassandra does not do this automatically. Otherwise you will end up with increased disk utilization over time. A logical time to remove incremental backups is on creation of a new snapshot or after you have moved them to an off-site location.

Restoring from a snapshot

Unfortunately, the procedure to restore from a snapshot is less trivial than the initial snapshot creation process. Before starting the restore procedure, it is important to first truncate the table. If you fail to truncate the table, you will lose any data that was deleted after the backup occurred. This is because the tombstones written to cover that data will have higher timestamps than the restored data.

Restoring from backup can be accomplished in one of two ways:

- Shutting down the node, removing old commit logs and SSTables, copying the backups to the node, and then restarting the node
- Using the `sstableloader` utility to load the snapshot

Considering that the first option requires a significant amount of node downtime, we will focus on the second option. To restore using the `sstableloader` option, complete the following steps:

1. Copy the snapshots into a directory structure that matches the following pattern: `[keyspace]/[table]/[snapshots]`. This is a hard requirement for the tool to pick up the correct files.
2. Run the following command:

```
sstableloader -d host1,host2,host3 [keyspace]/[table]
```

Ideally, you should not run this operation from a Cassandra node, as the operation will consume significant resources on that node. Note that this process will stream data to the appropriate nodes, and the host list is simply a set of initial contact points. You can also run many of these loaders concurrently to reduce the overall load time. It is also possible to throttle the amount of bandwidth used by the `sstableloader` process by specifying the `-t` option.

Summary

Handling failure in a distributed system is non-trivial and requires extra vigilance on the part of the system designers. This is especially true in a stateful, coordinated database like Cassandra. Fortunately, the architects of Cassandra have done an excellent job in building a resilient, fault-tolerant system that is designed from the ground up to be highly available.

We have covered a lot of ground in this book, from the basics of distributed database design to building scalable Cassandra data models. While not exhaustive by any means, the topics covered have hopefully helped you gain confidence as you design and deploy your Cassandra-backed applications.

As you take the next step in your journey with Cassandra, please participate by sharing your experience and learning from others. The project has a strong community of individuals and businesses who are committed to building the most scalable and resilient database in the world, and we value contribution at any level.

Thank you for taking the time to read this book, and good luck as you build game-changing applications!

Index

E

EC2 snitch 51
Extract, Transform and Load (ETL) 54

F

failover 50, 51
failure detector 170

G

garbage collector logs 165
  reference link 165
geographic distribution 51, 52, 53, 54
geohashing 134
geospatial data
  querying 134
GossipingPropertyFileSnitch 61

H

Hadoop Distributed File System (HDFS) 55
Hadoop
  used, for online analysis 55, 56
hardware configuration
  principles, for selection 74, 75
  selecting 74, 75
hash table
  distributed hash table (DHT) 21, 22
  fundamentals 19, 20
hashing 14
heterogeneous nodes 31
hinted handoff 41

I

Integrated Development Environment (IDE) 89

J

Java Development Kit (JDK) 89, 160
Java Management Extensions (JMX)
  about 160
  reference link, for configuration 160
Java Virtual Machine (JVM) 160

L

latency outliers
  searching 168
leveled compaction
  about 113
  advantages 113
lists 125, 126
live backup 50
load balancing, policies
  DCAwareRoundRobinPolicy 96
  LatencyAwarePolicy 96
  RoundRobinPolicy 96
  TokenAwarePolicy 96
  WhiteListPolicy 96
load balancing
  about 51, 95, 96
  consistency level, downgrading 97, 98
  remote data center, failing over 96, 97
  token awareness 100, 101, 102
log-structured storage engine
  about 108
  implications 108
logging
  about 164
  Cassandra logs 164
  garbage collector logs 165

M

maps 125, 127
master-slave model
  about 10
  master failure, handling 12
  sharding, used to scale writes 11
materialized views
  about 128
  denormalization 129
memtable 108
monolithic architecture 8, 9
multi-key queries 140
multiple data centers
  consistency 65
  consistency, achieving 70
  replicated write, anatomy 67, 68, 69, 70
  use cases 50

Made in the USA
San Bernardino, CA
13 January 2019